HONG KONG CASES IN
HUMAN RESOURCES MANAGEMENT

D0843988

HONG KONG
— CASES IN —
HUMAN RESOURCES
MANAGEMENT

Compiled and edited by
The Management Development Centre of Hong Kong

The Chinese University Press

The Management Development Centre of Hong Kong

ISBN 962–201–740–1

THE CHINESE UNIVERSITY PRESS
The Chinese University of Hong Kong
Sha Tin, N.T., Hong Kong
Fax: +852 2603 6692
      +852 2603 7355
E-mail: cup@cuhk.edu.hk
Web-site: http://www.cuhk.edu.hk/cupress/w1.htm

Printed in Hong Kong

Contents

Preface

In 1987 the Management Development Centre of Hong Kong (MDC) realized that there was a serious shortage of locally relevant management cases for use by trainers and teachers in Hong Kong. It began, therefore, to encourage the writing of cases and published its first English language case compendium in early 1989. Since then, four other case compendia have appeared, including two Chinese language editions. These cases are widely used by educational institutions, training providers, and many companies for in-company management training.

In order to enable management trainers to use the cases more effectively, MDC in collaboration with The Chinese University Press has published a new series of Hong Kong case books for classroom use since 1996. All the cases included in the series are local ones, and can form the basis of a teaching or training session for groups or self-learning activities, and, of course, they may also be used as projects or exercises to identify development needs.

The Management Development Centre
of Hong Kong
December 1997

Introduction

What is a "case study"? It is a representation of reality. Usually, it is a problem taken from real life. Indeed, all of the cases in this book are based upon events that actually happened in Hong Kong.

Each case should contain sufficient background data for students to identify the issues and put forward proposed solutions. No case can, by its very nature, contain all the information needed for a perfect decision. However, that is itself like the world in which the practising manager has to live. Most managers operate in conditions of incomplete knowledge and can never be sure about the impact of their decisions. Moreover, decisions seldom prove to be "right" or "wrong." The situation that a manager faces is seldom that clear-cut.

Tackling a Case

If you are a student faced with a case study for the first time, this may look a pretty daunting task. You may be at a loss to know where to start. The guidelines below are by no means comprehensive but you should find them useful.

Step 1: Groundwork

Read the case through quickly to give yourself an idea of the "big picture." Re-read the case, marking what you consider to be the key areas or the areas about which you are uncertain.

Step 2: Problems

After a third reading, list down what you see as the main problem areas. Prioritize these problems:
1. Which are the most important?
2. Which are having the biggest impact and why?
3. Which demand the most immediate attention and why?

Step 3: Analysis

1. How did the problems occur? What are the causes?
2. Do not fall into the trap of confusing symptoms with core problems.
3. Where you do not have sufficient information, make assumptions that you can rationally defend.
4. Most fundamentally, are all these problems actually capable of solution?

Step 4: Alternatives

Most problems can be tackled and "solved" in a number of different ways. Generate possible courses of action and test them by asking yourself:

1. How many of the problems will this solve?
2. To what extent will they be solved?
3. Will this solve the most important, most basic problem(s)?
4. What resources will this course of action require? Are they available?
5. Are there any disadvantages to this solution? What are the risks?

Step 5: Action

Which course of action is the "best"? Be sure that you are explicit about what makes it "best." Is it speed, economy, acceptability?

Draw up your plan answering these questions:

1. *What* is going to be done?
2. *Who* is going to do it?
3. *When* is it going to be done and what are the stages along the way?
4. *How* is it going to be done? Set down the detail of your approach.
5. *Why* is it going to be done that way?

If you follow these steps and can answer these questions, you are probably well on the way to an effective case solution.

Step 6: Confirmation

A useful check, when you have completed your work on the case, is to go through the following process.

Findings	Conclusions	Recommendations
1.	1.	1.
2.	2.	2.
3.	3.	3.
4.	4.	
5.	5.	
6.		
7.		
8.		

1. List your findings, the information that you have gathered about the situation described in the case.
2. Write down your conclusions based on your findings. Each conclusion *must* be based on your findings. You cannot make conclusions that are not backed up by *facts*.
3. Draft your recommendations for action. Every one of your recommendations *has to be* supported by at least one of your conclusions.

In the diagram, Recommendation 1 is backed by Conclusion 1. However, Conclusion 1 is not based on findings. Hence, it is not being supported.

Part I

Introduction to Human Resources Management

1

Asian Arts Centre

Christina Lee

So much was on Eva's mind as she parked off her car at the Asian Arts Centre, the prestigious cultural venue she manages. So many questions ran through her mind for which she could find no easy answers. "Am I ineffective? Inefficient? Not hardworking enough? Or according to Peter's Principle, have I been promoted to my level of incompetence? What have I done wrong? How come nothing are working right?" As she took the lift to her luxurious office, she reflected upon how these problems had started.

Eva was a high flyer. She started working in the Cultural Branch of the Municipal Government six years ago as an Assistant Manager in Cultural Programmes Unit. As a piano player, she was very familiar with classical music. She was therefore particularly motivated when she was assigned to the Concerts subsection. She did a great job there, and at the same time enjoyed herself by meeting renowned musicians from around the world. Within a relatively short time of two-and-a-half years, compared to an average of four, she had been promoted to the grade of manager.

However, to her initial disappointment, she was posted to the District Arts Centres Planning Unit. Her job was to plan for the new smaller district arts centres in the municipality. Principally, she liaised and coordinated requirements with all relevant parties including end-users, architects, engineers, suppliers and so forth. The work seemed a little baffling at the beginning, but after much hard work and determination, she was performing very well and earned the praise of the senior management. Her supervisor, being very busy himself, was particularly appreciative of her ability to work independently. In three-and-a-half years, with the successful opening of the last district arts centre under planning, Eva was promoted to the rank of senior manager. She was a little overwhelmed, because no one had ever been promoted to that rank with only six years' experience in the grade and at such a young age (she was only 29). Nonetheless she was very pleased with herself and was determined to do even better in her new and prestigious post. She was also aware that the senior management had high expectation and promised herself that she would not let anyone down.

The first day she went to the new office, the Chief Executive, Albert Kwong, came down from the Head Office to introduce her to her team. There were Sam, the Administration Manager, and his Assistant Managers, Sarah, Willy and Dominic. There were Ruby, the Operations Manager, and her Assistant Managers, Tony, Ada, Candy and Beatrice. There were Joseph, the Booking and Promotion Manager, and his Assistant Managers, Coco, Leon and Amanda (see Figure 1).

Albert congratulated Eva on her brilliant work in the past and said that he was confident to make the Asian Arts Centre an even more sought-after venue for cultural events. He mentioned in passing that her predecessor, who had resigned, was not doing that well. "Without good management," he added, "this beautiful work of art in itself will be wasted. Eva, it's all yours." And after giving her a briefing which lasted no more than 20 minutes, he left her office and was subsequently seen only on two occasions during the opening parties before two performances. In fact, in many times, Eva had thought of turning to Albert for advice but backed off because she told herself that being able to work with minimum supervision was what she was known for.

For the first four weeks, Eva stayed in the office daily from 8 in the morning till 11 at night, studying files, getting to know more than 100 staff members, meeting clients, hirers, contractors, suppliers etc., understanding how everything worked, and familiarizing herself with the venue itself.

She admitted to herself that previously she had been totally oblivious to the whole spectrum of knowledge relating to venue management. For the first time, her confidence was undermined. The

Figure 1: Organization Structure of Asian Arts Centre

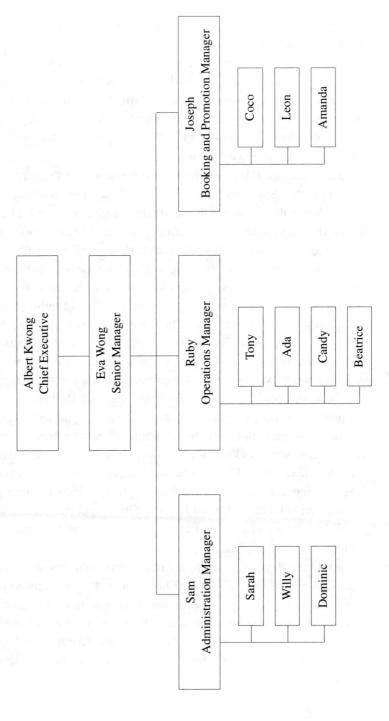

prospect of having to manage so many people, many elder than herself and more experienced, nearly overwhelmed her.

Physically tired by her first weeks on-the-job, they were in reality a honeymoon period compared with what was to follow. The problems just never seemed to stop. Six months after taking up the job she was ashamed to tell people how little she had achieved. What was she supposed to have achieved anyway? She had no idea and so she could only react when problems arose.

Well, for one thing, she had come to know her three managers a little bit better. Sam was a hardworking fellow. He was always the last one to leave the office at night, staying sometimes until 11.30 p.m. Every time Eva visited Sam's office, he was always working away, either looking up manuals and procedures, or writing up file notes or reports which Eva found irritating to read because they were unnecessary and full of grammatical mistakes. Eva tried to tell him that some of the reports were not really needed but fell short of telling him about the numerous mistakes he made because she respected Sam as a kind and conscientious man. She knew his unit was working on a number of rectification projects, among which was a backstage water leakage problem at the Lyric Theatre. Numerous tests had been carried out and yet the cause could not be determined. Michael Holbert, the project architect, had been a number of times to investigate and explain the mechanics to Sam, but Sam always wanted Eva to be present no matter how routine the check-up was. Among other reasons why Eva was unwilling to entertain Sam was because of her intolerance of his spoken English. She did not even want him to greet Holbert because he was always saying Hofat instead of Holbert. She did not correct him because she did not want to hurt him. Besides, how many more words could she correct?

And then there was Sarah, the newly recruited Assistant Manager. The blunders she made during her first month at work included letting a maintenance team carry out a routine investigation of the stage during a dress rehearsal, authorizing time-off for half of the backstage crew on the same day, among others. Subsequently, Eva assigned Sarah to Ruby's team, and appointed Beatrice, who was more experienced, to help out Sam.

The swapping of posts made Ruby very unhappy. Already, she thought she was looking after an important area in the centre. She should be given the best people instead. Now, she thought, she had to supervise yet another dumb person. Ruby was very intelligent. She had a Master's degree in Arts Administration and thought highly of herself. She was sharp in identifying and solving problems in operations and proficient in technical aspects of theatre management. But at least three times in the last four months, Eva had received complaints from customers about Ruby's arrogance. When Eva talked to Ruby about this, Ruby dismissed the complaints as a nuisance, attributed them to the customers' ignorance of technical knowledge and unreasonable demands. She even suggested that Eva's relationship with the customers was too close, in a way encouraging them to complain. At first, Eva thought Ruby could teach Sarah a few things. Now she was not so sure. Well, what about Joseph?

Joseph was the most senior in terms of age and experience. He knew the ropes well enough. He had a wide network of connections and was very resourceful. He maintained a solid performance but somehow, Eva had a feeling that Joseph could do more. Apparently, he could not care less! He was concerned about getting his, and only his, work done during normal office hours. Eva had never seen him at the office after 5 p.m. Not that she thought that overtime was necessary in order to be effective. It was his attitude of not caring about things that bothered Eva. Coco, one of his Assistant Managers, and the most "artistic" among all staff, was consistently late for work. She was also known to be writing her own contributions to magazines during office hours. However, Joseph said it did not affect her normal work. Eva had a feeling that Joseph did not want to lose Coco's contacts with friends in communications. It was fortunate that the other two team members, Leon and Amanda, were not really concerned about that. In fact, the two had quite a few good ideas for promoting the centre. Eva spent time discussing them at length and had worked out a great proposal for senior management, only to be told that no resources were available. That was a blow to Eva and an even greater blow to Leon and Amanda. They had pinned a lot of hopes on the proposal because previously, their ideas had never got past Joseph.

The other day, Eva got an urgent memo from Albert asking her to prepare detailed statistics on booking rates, operating costs and expenditure profiles as well as a revenue statement. She had heard that the other big cultural centre across the harbour had been closely questioned by the Municipal Council two months ago on its low booking rates and huge operating costs. Now, it must be her turn! But that was not the only external problem she faced.

Officers from the Audit Department had recently spent two weeks studying files and observing her staff at work. She was doubtful that Sam's unnecessary reports and Coco's lax behaviour would have escaped their careful scrutiny. Besides Sam and Coco, there could be others who were not doing the "proper" things in the office, or not doing them in the "proper" way. She knew all too well that somebody would have to bear the brunt when these "improprieties" were brought to the attention of the City High Council in the Annual Audit Report. Unfortunately she just did not have the time to check everything out in the centre. To her, it was already an achievement to be able to remember the names of most of the people there.

With all these issues on her mind, Eva walked into the office only to find Sam already there. "Mr. Hofat will be here at 9 o'clock. Can you talk to him?" Sam said. "I've also got a progress report on the leakage problem for you to check. It's okay if you amend it."

"Oh no! Another morning devoted solely to Sam!" She lamented to herself. Just then, Tony walked in. "Eva, Sarah is crying in the washroom …"

Questions for Discussion

Approach 1: Syndicate Discussion for Performance Management Training

The class can be divided into small groups of 4–6 people. Each participant should read the entire case individually. Then each group should focus their discussion on one or more characters assigned by the trainer. Suggested groups are as follows:

1. A class with 5 groups

- Group 1 to focus on Eva
- Group 2 to focus on Sam
- Group 3 to focus on Ruby and Coco
- Group 4 to focus on Joseph
- Group 5 to focus on Sarah and Albert

2. A class with 4 groups
   - Group 1 to focus on Eva
   - Group 2 to focus on Sam
   - Group 3 to focus on Ruby, Sarah and Albert
   - Group 4 to focus on Joseph and Coco

3. A class with 3 groups
   - Group 1 to focus on Eva and Albert
   - Group 2 to focus on Sam and Coco
   - Group 3 to focus on Ruby, Sarah and Joseph

The group task is to analyse the case and:
1. list all the performance problems for the character(s) assigned;
2. suggest reasons for these problems; and
3. suggest how they would address these problems from
   a. Eva's point of view; and
   b. the centre's point of view.

Approach 2: Discussion Questions for Communication Training

Individually or in groups of 4–6 people, participants should review the following questions and discuss:
1. communications among the staff of the Asian Arts Centre,
2. how communications (or lack of it) have affected the performance of individuals in the centre as well as the performance of the centre as a whole,
3. how, as a communications consultant hired by the centre, they would improve the current situation.

Approach 3: Human Resources Management Concept Training

Trainees need to be familiar with human resources management issues including management development, career planning, performance management and training and development before they can attempt this approach to the case.

Individually, or in groups of 4–6 people, participants should attempt the following questions and discuss their views:

1. Has Eva been over-promoted? Give reasons to support your view.
2. If you were the senior management, how could you have prepared Eva for her new appointment?
3. What are your views on the career development of Joseph, Sam and Ruby?
4. How could Eva better manage the performance of her staff?

Part II

Human Resources Planning

Siu Chong Clothing Factory Limited

K. F. Chan and Theresa Lau

Factory History

The Siu Chong Clothing Factory Limited is one of the oldest, traditional family-type clothing manufacturing companies in Hong Kong. It has been trading for thirty years and employs around one hundred workers who perform the main production functions. In addition, there are ten office staff providing administrative and management support for the whole operation.

In the 1960s, the founder Sam Lo rented a small factory in Sham Shui Po and started a small clothing operation making traditional blouses and shirts which were destined mainly for overseas markets. Low labour costs and a diligent labour force contributed to the success of the factory and business grew steadily.

The present Managing Director Keith Mak, Lo's brother-in-law, feels that when the factory was first set up, the lack of competition, and low levels of import restriction abroad, helped make the factory successful. However, in the past five years the company has only managed to achieve annual growth in output levels of 10–15%. Total production last year amounted to 35 million pieces.

To enable the factory to expand its production capacity and better control rental costs, Siu Chong moved to new premises at the Kwun Tong industrial estate. The new factory provides a relatively modern, spacious and comfortable environment. Nearly all the machinery has been imported from West Germany and Japan, and Mak intends to keep abreast of technology by replacing machinery every three to four years.

Lo is now in his sixties and is preparing to emigrate to Canada after gradually handing over the business to Mak.

Mak has a Diploma in Mechanical Engineering from Hong Kong Polytechnic. After graduation, he worked as a mechanical engineer onboard ship for ten years. Before he took over the factory, he worked as a Planning Engineer for China Light and Power for two years.

Mak had intended to continue running the factory the way it has always been operated. However, he began to realize that the traditional operating style was restrictive and decided to introduce a more systematic approach to managing the business. Lo is always away from Hong Kong and he only keeps in touch with Mak on critical management decisions. In practice, Mak has complete autonomy over the company's daily operations.

The Current Situation

Like many other garment firms in Hong Kong, Siu Chong is mainly an export-oriented company. Its largest market is West Germany. Ladies' blouses and shirts are made to meet overseas buyers' specifications. For over ten years, the factory has maintained a very close relationship with a single big buyer. Nearly 99% of annual sales are derived from the orders of one German company which modifies the packs, labels and prices of Siu Chong's products for the German market.

The founder of Siu Chong originally established the connection with the German buyer, and Mak is well aware that it is risky to rely on one client. He is hoping to increase his customer base but has no real idea how to do so. The factory has not advertised in the media, and most of their customers are obtained from enquires and referrals through the government's Industry and Trade Departments.

Most of the orders come in spring and winter. Regular orders, spread throughout the year, make up a very small proportion of the factory's sales. If rush orders occur, the factory subcontracts part of the job to smaller manufacturers in Hong Kong. Sometimes poor workmanship and labour shortages cause late deliveries to clients.

The ladies' blouses and shirts produced by Siu Chong are traditional and basic. They are not subject to changes in fashion, so it is unnecessary to set up a design department. Any changes in colour and style are specified by clients.

From Mak's experience, there is only moderate competition in this sector of the market. He feels that because the factory has maintained its export quota, and staff have worked hard, the factory has maintained a steady growth pattern of around 10% in the last few years. This was achieved at a time when other companies were closing their operations or moving to China to reduce labour costs.

Organization Structure

The company has no formal organization chart. The division of work is based on experience and the production work flow. Figure 1 represents the organization structure drawn up from the rough ideas presented by Keith Mak. The numbers in parentheses denote the number of employees in each activity.

The factory covers approximately 10,000 square feet. This is divided into two main parts: a small administrative office and a large workshop area. The workshop has about 100 workers handling "pressing" work.

Figure 1: Organization Structure of Siu Chong Clothing Factory

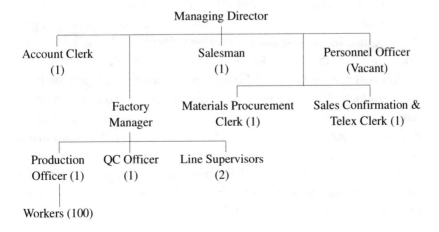

Factory workers are skilful and have been with the company for a long time. Unfortunately it is now becoming increasingly difficult to recruit younger, reliable workers. It is anticipated that labour turnover will get more serious in the near future.

The overall administrative and management systems of the factory are simple. There are no formal rules and regulations monitoring workers' conduct, responsibilities, working conditions, benefits, and so on. After taking over the management of the factory, Mak found that he has difficulty in handling labour disputes. There were no written standards or rules for reference. Traditionally, the company had emphasized "loyalty" and "good relations." Mak has arranged a series of social activities, such as picnics, barbecues, festival celebrations and short trips to Southeast Asian countries.

Siu Chong operates on the basis of informality. Working relations are built on trust, and this appears to work well even though there are no discussions between management and workers. In the past the factory had been so small that formal rules and procedures seemed unnecessary. However, workers' attitudes, competition, the labour market and political environment all are changing and some sort of system must be introduced if the company is to continue to survive.

The Problems and the Changes

Although the impact of labour shortages on the factory are not as serious as in similar companies in the same industry, the factory is not without its problems. In the first place, overall profits are declining because of fluctuations in the Hong Kong dollar exchange rate. Secondly, the market is shrinking because of quota restrictions and competition from other products. Too much reliance on one customer, and lack of product innovation are also having an adverse affect. Not only are there no design staff, but there are also no plans to recruit any. The third major issue is that the factory has clearly shown that it is not always capable of meeting its deadlines. Late deliveries damage long-term customer relationships. In addition, staff shortages have meant squeezing more overtime hours out of workers and in this situation, it has been difficult to control the quality of work done. Rising labour costs represent another problem.

Given these problems Mak has decided to implement certain measures to protect the future of the business. His first initiative was to draft a document — Employment Contract — setting out the rules and regulations governing terms and conditions of employment. This document is reproduced in Appendix 1. Mak believes that it will help to solve the labour disputes, clarify work responsibilities and minimize arguments among workers.

Mak's second decision was to offer more social activities for staff which, he feels, will help to improve worker-management relations.

The third development is a new superannuation fund for the workers. Both the staff and the company are required to contribute to the fund but the workers' contribution is much less than that of the company. It is claimed that this scheme is unique among small firms in the clothing industry and that by adopting it worker loyalty and morale will be enhanced.

Mak also considered dismissing his pressing workers and replace them with contract staff. The main objective here is to make the factory more flexible and responsive to change.

Mak has also focused on administration and planning in the company. He is very keen to install personal computers to help reduce administrative workloads. In particular, he wants them to be used in production planning, materials purchasing and accounting. Computerization will significantly improve efficiency but clearly the capability of staff must also be considered.

Appendix 1: Employment Contract

1. Every new employee must complete a Company Employee Particulars Form.
2. Employees will be notified of their normal working hours on appointment. Section heads may require staff to work overtime whenever necessary. Should an employee not comply with the Company's instructions to work overtime on more than two

working days within one wage period, the individual may forfeit the incentive bonus for that wage period.

3. New employees paid on a monthly basis are subject to a probation period of three months. This probation may be extended at the Company's discretion. After the probation period, the Company may confirm employment subject to satisfactory performance. For sewing workers, the probation period is seven days.

4. Employment may be terminated by either party with written notice. Resignation shall be submitted through the head of the section to which an employee is attached. The following regulations shall govern matters regarding prior written notice or payment in lieu of notice should the employee or the Company wishes to terminate employment:

   a. Within the first month of the probation period, the employee or the Company may at any time terminate the employment without notice or payment in lieu;

   b. After the first months of a probation period, if employment has not been confirmed, the employee or Company may terminate employment on seven days' written notice, or seven days' payment in lieu of written notice;

   c. After the confirmation of employment, the employee or Company may thereafter terminate the employment.

5. Termination of Service by the Company

   The Company may terminate the contract of employment of an employee without prior written notice or payment in lieu if such termination is due to employee fraud, dishonesty, or wilful disobedience of a lawful and reasonable order.

6. As an incentive scheme to attract more recruits, new sewing workers will be given a bonus equal to 20% of wages earned in their first wage period, and 10% of wages earned in their second wage period. A bonus of HK$500 is payable upon completion of three months' service.

7. Maternity Leave

   A female employee who has worked for the Company for a period of not less than 26 weeks is entitled to maternity leave. The employee must give the Company notice of intention to take maternity leave at least 12 weeks in advance of the expected date of confinement.

The employee is entitled to pay during the four weeks' leave taken immediately prior to the expected date of confinement and the six weeks' leave taken immediately after confinement, or for a fixed period of sixty days. The pay rate is two-thirds of her average daily wage during the month immediately preceding leave, excluding incentive bonus, travelling allowance, overtime pay and allowances.

A female employee forfeits her entitlement to maternity leave pay if she works, without the permission of the Company, for another employer during her maternity leave.

8. Overtime Payment

Overtime up to	Overtime payment (hourly rate)
On weekdays:	
8:00 p.m.	HK$ 6.00
9:00 p.m.	HK$11.00
10:00 p.m.	HK$16.00
	plus 20% of the daily wage
11:00 p.m.	HK$21.00
	plus 20% of the daily wage
On Sunday & public holidays:	
9:00 a.m.–5:00 p.m.	HK$16.00

9. Sickness Allowance

An employee who has worked continuously for the Company for a period of one month preceding his sickness is entitled to sickness allowance. The maximum accumulated paid sickness days are subject to the provisions of the Employment Ordinance of Hong Kong.

The daily rate of sickness allowance is equal to two-thirds of the average daily wages for thirteen days immediately prior to leave, excluding incentive bonus, travelling allowance, overtime payment and allowances.

An employee is not entitled to sickness allowance if:

a. the sick leave is less than four days;

b. he/she fails to produce a medical certificate from a registered doctor;

c. his/her unfitness for work is caused by his/her serious and wilful misconduct;

d. his/her sickness day falls on a statutory holiday on which he/she is entitled to pay.

Every day off for a female employee to have pregnancy check-ups or post-confinement medical treatment should be taken as sick leave and be paid at two-thirds of her normal wages, excluding allowances and overtime pay.

10. Piece-rate employees must submit all job order stubs to their section head at the end of each working day for the calculation of wages. Should the Company find that an employee intentionally accumulates stubs and presents them at a later date, the employee may forfeit his incentive bonus and allowances for that wage period.

11. The Company may, at its discretion, amend the terms or conditions contained in this Employment Contract. Changes will be notified to employees in writing.

Questions for Discussion

1. With reference to the company's operational environment, comment on the organization structure formulated by the Managing Director.

2. What problems do you think may arise if Keith Mak implements the changes he proposes? In particular, what difficulties may arise with the employment contract and superannuation fund?

3. Analyse the impact on company operations and performance of replacing the pressing workers with contract staff.

4. Do you agree with the overall approach that the company intends to use to cope with the problems it faces? Justify your answers.

3

What to Do?

Maureen Chan

"Good morning, Ms. Wong," Mei-yee's colleague greeted her as she walked slowly to her workplace. Mei-yee was surprised by her indifference, as her colleague was already an hour late for work. She really did not know what to do.

Wong Mei-yee, who has been working for the Happy Travel Company for over ten years, was promoted to Human Resources Manager a year ago. Over the year, she has faced a very embarrassing situation which she does not know how to handle. The problem of staff punctuality has become worse and the top management continued to urge her to do something about it. The general situation was getting still worse. A few days ago, the passports of ten customers were lost and there were no clues as to who was responsible. The main issue is that Mei-yee cannot have a clear picture on who has entered the office and at what time. The problems of punctuality and the loss of passports seemed to be two separate issues, but they both reflect the shortfall, maybe some common problems, of the human resources systems, many of which have been implemented for a long time without any change. In order to know the root causes for the problems, Mei-yee has to reconsider the various aspects of human resources policies and systems in her company. She starts from reviewing the historical and business development of the company.

The business was started up in 1970s by a couple, who are the Director and General Manager of the company. The travel business is growing fast as travel has become a favourite pastime among Hong

Kong people. The family business also has grown and now has 300 employees. The main business is outbound tours. It operates tours all over the world and has now over 80 different kinds of tour. Ticketing and inbound tours are some other businesses which are gaining importance. There are eight departments at the headquarters, namely Inbound Tours; Ticketing; Outbound Tours; Finance and Administration; Human Resources; Visas; Marketing and Promotion; and Customer Services. In addition to the departments in the headquarters, there are thirteen branches for retailing functions all around Hong Kong.

Mei-yee reports directly to the General Manager, and it is up to her to handle all matters related to personnel. When Mei-yee joined the company ten years ago, there were only 20 persons. She could easily get to know the staff very well. As the business has developed into an enterprise with an increasing number of employees, she can hardly recognize the face of every member of staff. Moreover, the situation gets worse when the company recruits freelance escorts during the peak months, normally during the holiday seasons. Then the office is crowded with new faces. The freelance escorts can move around the office freely.

She is now wondering whether she can raise this difficult situation with the General Manager who seems to sympathize with Mei-yee quite a lot.

As the company's Human Resources Manager, Mei-yee strongly believes that equity is the key principle in good human resources management and especially staff compensation. The office hours are from 9:00 a.m. to 5:30 p.m. for the back office and every member of staff should know that from their first day at work. She thinks that all back office staff should start work at 9:00 a.m. However, one department always breaks this rule, namely the Marketing and Promotion Department. There they tend to adopt a flexitime working system, and the staff comes to office an hour or even two hours late. Owing to the nature of the business, most of the staff are young. Most are under thirty. And when some staff find others always coming to work late without censure, they simply follow suit.

Fully realizing the serious effect this problem may have, Mei-yee goes to see the Marketing and Promotion Manager, Jenny, hoping to find a solution and resolve the problem. Jenny explains, "My staff always needs to stay late in the evening to finish up the design work for the promotional materials for the next day. They have pressure from the top to come out with high-quality and timely designs. They sometimes even stay in the office overnight to complete the job. I can hardly complain to them when they only come to work one or two hours late as a way to keep up their spirits for next day's heavy workload. Can you tell me what I should do?" Although Mei-yee understands the difficulty and pressure faced by the Marketing and Promotion Department, she still thinks that staff should be at work on time. Most designers are highly paid. They are not compensated for working late. But after all, this policy applies to all the other managerial grade staff in the company too.

As one of the major local travel companies, it has a large customer base. However, the competition is fierce, since many local companies have joined the business. The travel business fluctuates with the seasonal holidays, and timely advertising is their most important promotional tool. They need to put advertisements in the newspaper without delay, and top management puts a lot of emphasis on the quality and timely promotions of their tours. It appreciates the efforts made by the Marketing and Promotion staff. Mei-yee, as a result, cannot take too strict an approach to deal with this staff problem.

Mei-yee circulates a memo to the staff to note the importance of punctuality. The situation does not change much. The general situation becomes more difficult to deal with when ten passports were lost and no one is found to be responsible. In practice, every departmental manager has one set of keys for the office door. They take turns to open the door every morning. They are free to arrange to have someone in their department to keep the key. When the door is opened every morning, the staff can enter the office freely. During the last few days, many departments, including the Visas, Tours and Customer Services Departments have worked late in the evening.

Mei-yee realizes the need to do something, otherwise incidents of losing passports may occur again. Although she always explains to the staff in her department why they have to be punctual, her staff feel a bit confused when other colleagues do not keep to the same rule. What do you think Mei-yee can do in this critical situation?

Questions for Discussion

1. Is equity the most important principle in rewarding staff?
2. What kinds of human resources problems are Mei-yee facing?
3. What factors have led to these problems?
4. What can Mei-yee do to solve the problems she is facing?

Part III

Staffing, Orientation
and Placement

4

Training Scheme Failure

Lesley Watt

Background

Hong Kong Paging and Hong Kong Mobile Phone belong to the same telecommunications company group. Although they belong to the same mother company, each operates on its own. For example, they have different marketing strategies, and personnel and administration policies.

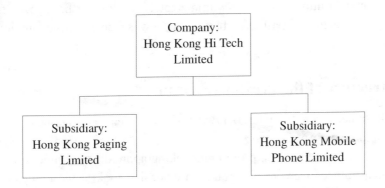

In 1996, the group believed that it was right time to rationalize and bring the two companies together to achieve greater efficiency, better utilization of resources and most importantly, a clearer image for its customers in the global marketplace. This situation had arisen because competition was becoming keener not only from local companies but also from companies in general in the region. Furthermore, customers had become more demanding as their expectations rose. If the group was to continue its former success, Hong Kong had to be kept as a centre, and to achieve all of these things, group restructuring had become essential.

Before the restructuring exercise took place, both companies had their own trainee schemes which had been running for five years. The objective of these schemes was to provide newly recruited tertiary graduates with comprehensive training and job experience in a wide range of company activities with the emphasis on developing professionals in certain particular disciplines, e.g. finance, marketing and personnel management. When running independently, both schemes had enjoyed a good reputation locally and had attracted a number of bright candidates each year.

After the restructuring exercise, many of the departments with similar functions were merged — the training departments of both companies being no exception. Redundancy in many departments was inevitable. Mary Lee was the training manager of Hong Kong Paging and in charge of its trainee scheme there. After merging the training departments, it was her task to develop a group trainee scheme and to start recruitment of trainees immediately. Following her successful experience in the past, she based the new scheme on the previous scheme.

Structure of the Previous Scheme

All trainees were to undergo a two-and-a-half-year programme divided into three parts as follows:

Part I was an initial programme taking approximately nine months when trainees were to undertake an extensive look at the company's various activities.

This part included an intensive induction to the ten divisions (Sales, Marketing, Sales Support, Customer Care, Network Engineering, Network Design, Human Resources, Public Relations, Finance, and Operations). Although the trainee was recruited for a particular discipline, attendance of the whole training course organized by the training department was compulsory.

After satisfactorily completing Part I, trainees commenced the nine-month Part II training period, when trainees were given an in-depth appreciation of the work of the departments working closely with their chosen discipline. Project work was included, and trainees were rotated to various departments for periods of four to six weeks at a time.

The twelve-month Part III training course commenced upon the satisfactory completion of Part II training. This advanced training was aimed at training in the chosen discipline in which the trainee would work upon completion of the whole training course. Upon satisfactory completion, the departmental manager submitted a recommendation for the trainee as appointment to his department and obtained the requisite approval from the Head of the Division.

During the entire period of training, progress reports were prepared by the departmental managers or their nominated staff and forwarded to the training department.

The scheme was supported by all the departments, as they welcomed the continuous supply of front-line executives trained on the scheme. Compared with any qualified and experienced external recruits, trainees from the scheme had the advantage of understanding the organization better, connecting with their colleagues better and possibly identifying with the company more strongly.

The trainees were also satisfied with the scheme, as their career path was more secure and steady progress was made possible. This was supported by the fact that the average trainee turnover rate was under 10%.

On a personal level, Mary had been with the company for ten years and had already established a very good relationship with the line managers. It was, therefore, easy for her to obtain support from them.

Based on her experience in running the previous trainee scheme, she used the same framework for the new scheme and was confident that it would work out effectively.

The New Scheme

After the restructuring exercise, instead of recruiting trainees for all the disciplines as before, only trainees for marketing and sales were to be recruited, as these were the only areas to be expanded.

Mary, accordingly, worked out a training schedule and made the necessary arrangements with the various departments. At the same time, the recruitment of trainees was taking place. The new scheme attracted numerous applicants and finally twenty were recruited. The aim was to equip these new recruits with managerial skills and professional knowledge through an intensive and comprehensive training programme for the marketing and sales departments to fill their new manpower needs.

The scheme started well but as time went by, problems began to occur. After Part I training, Mary had difficulty in finding relevant departments to provide specialized training for the trainees. The departments were reluctant to provide training opportunities for the trainees, as they saw this as an investment with no obvious return for them. In the past, most departments had had the opportunity to have trainees as permanent members of their staff upon completion of their Part III training. It now seemed that they were only helping the marketing and sales sections to train their people. Given the very tight resources after the restructuring exercise, some departments were hardly enthusiastic about the trainee scheme. Others, however, did welcome the trainees as supplying an extra hand given the very tight headcount situation.

When, however, the final specialized training had been arranged and begun, other problems occurred. Some departments that were willing to provide training opportunities complained that the trainees were not particularly cooperative and they did not want to take up the more routine jobs. The trainees also complained that they were either being assigned to very administrative or merely clerical duties, or were just treated as an extra pair of helping hands providing them with no really new learning experience. Departments explained that with attachments of only four to six weeks, it was difficult to assign them to any important tasks.

Positive and negative statements were heard:

"My supervisor is a very experienced and professional manager. During my attachment in his department, he let me handle the organization of a mini exhibition. The experience has helped me improve my planning, organization and interpersonal skills. My supervisor also gave me very constructive feedback," said Tommy Chan, a trainee of the scheme.

"I found the attachment meaningless, as I was just given very operational tasks to do, for example, updating a customer database. Nothing new was learnt," said Helen Wong, a trainee of the scheme.

"The trainee attached to my department has made very good contribution. I let him handle the telesales project and very good results were produced within a short period of time," said David Cheung, a line manager.

Three of the trainees resigned from the scheme during the training period. The remaining seventeen finally completed the scheme but half of them were dissatisfied with the placement.

Although not all the cases were negative, the implementation and result of the new trainee scheme did not work out as Mary intended and she was very disappointed.

Questions for Discussion

1. Why did a scheme which worked well previously did not work equally well for the group company?
2. How should the scheme have been designed to suit the new situation?

5

Do-It-Yourself Body Shop

C. Lok

Introduction

Philip Wong wondered how he had gotten himself into this situation. He was successful in his career as a pharmacist in Tuen Mun Hospital. After considerable research and effort, he has successfully launched a new business venture along with his partner, Andrew Ma. The venture had initially gone very well for them since the opening of their first Do-It-Yourself (DIY) Body Shop Store eighteen months ago. A second store was opened six months ago. Although the initial success of the first store had encouraged them to open the second one, Philip was now wondering if that had been a mistake.

While Andrew Ma had managed the first store, the partners had hired a manager to run the second store. Unfortunately, he was ineffective and the partners were forced to dismiss him. Now both partners are managing the stores, while Philip continues to work full-time at the hospital. The hours were taking their toll on him and he knew that the business was at a crucial stage. He and Andrew had to decide whether to hire a new manager for the second store or to fold the second store and consolidate the first operation.

They decided that they needed help and enlisted the expertise of a management consultant, Joe Chan, to assist them in making the decision. Joe Chan met with both partners and they outlined the circumstances of the present situation.

Background to DIY Body Shop

Up until a year before opening the first store, Philip did not really know much about the DIY idea for selling toiletries (e.g. shampoo, soap, lotion). Like other consumers, he had purchased his toiletries at Watson's and Mannings stores paying $60–80 each time for a month's supply. Soon he discovered a new store in Tuen Mun that allowed customers to bottle their own shampoo, soap from bulk ingredients, at a substantially reduced cost. This caught Philip's imagination and after several months of research, Philip and his partner Andrew opened the first DIY Body Shop.

DIY Operations

After the initial success of the first store in Sha Tin, Philip and Andrew opened the second shop in Tai Po. The operation of the stores is simple. Customers, under the guidance of the shop staff, select the ingredient materials of the product and bottle them. The actual savings are in the region of 40–50% when compared with branded products of the same quality.

The Birth of the First DIY Store

Philip and Andrew decided to invest in setting up their first store two years ago. With bank loans and some personal savings, they spent $500,000 on everything needed to open the business. The store is located in Shatin Plaza near a railway station. After sending out flyers to a number of nearby housing estates, business took off. Many people were curious to see how a certain kind of product (e.g. shampoo) was made.

Philip found that customer education was the biggest key to success. From a marketing perspective, making customers knowledgeable about the features of a particular ingredient was advantageous as they would then likely purchase more. Educating customers was also advantageous from a practical point of view. When customers returned and became more familiar with selecting and mixing their own product, the staff will only provide information when requested by the customers.

Staffing at DIY

A team of "Personal Care Advisers" were necessary to help customers select the kind of ingredients that meet their personal needs. Philip and Andrew were not concerned that the applicants had previous "personal care" experience. The process of filling the bottles was quite straightforward. Personal Care Advisers could be trained quickly so that they were ready to guide customers within a week of starting their job.

As the partners gained more experience with the first store, they realized that not all Advisers were equally skilled in dealing with customers. Some were not skilful at conveying information to customers in an appropriate fashion; some literally did the blending for customers without explaining anything; others explained everything no matter how many times the customer had visited the store.

From the feedback of customers who filled out a questionnaire about the shop, the partners read comments like, "The product is great but I am sometimes made to feel like an idiot when I ask a question." Another comment indicated that a customer felt that he was "10 years old and back in primary five."

The partners tried to deal with these issues with staff at meetings and by encouraging the Advisers to "do better." However, no specific training was given to staff in this regard and negative comments continued to appear though with a reduced frequency.

The most important failure of the partners seemed to have been the hiring of a manager for their second store. Both Philip and Andrew had been impressed with the abilities of John Li, one of their Personal Care Advisers at the first location. He had a real talent for educating customers without talking down to them. Both partners valued this ability very highly; when they decided to open the second store, they both felt John was the person to manage it.

However, after several months, it was clear that although John possessed strong customer skills, he had never really managed a business before. The first hint of trouble occurred when John called frantically from the store one day saying that he had forgotten to order more ingredients and that he was coming to pick up what he needed from the first store.

The need for John's dismissal became clear when numerous customers complained that the ingredients were wrongly labelled. As a result, customers were not getting what they were paying for. When Andrew looked into these problems, he discovered the administrative mess that John had created.

Question for Discussion

As Joe Chan, identify and assess the human resources issues facing DIY and make recommendations.

6

The Success
Executive Trainees' Programme

Y. C. Chan

In 1995, one of the largest Japanese retail groups, the Success Group, decided to start operations in Hong Kong. Fifteen months before the opening of the store, the senior management of the Success Group carefully selected thirty-six Hong Kong graduates from the universities, whom they intended to train in the Japanese way to become the backbone of the Hong Kong operation in future. The Success Group invested over HK$10 million in this training programme, which was considered to be a substantial investment by the company.

At the beginning, the senior management chose a group of fresh local graduates from various disciplines who had one thing in common — a good command of the Japanese language. Nevertheless, they were chosen not only because of the need to use the language, but also because of their knowledge of Japanese culture. Some even had experience of living in Japan before they joined the company.

The main objective of selecting trainees with a knowledge of Japan was to train them to fully accept the Japanese way of management and corporate culture. They were first given a three months' intensive training course in the following areas: retail business, the Japanese language, and an introduction to the traditions and management culture of the Success Group. After three months, thirty-three of the trainees signed a two-year contract with the company and were sent to Japan for further training.

In Hong Kong, the training emphasized the theoretical aspects of retailing. In Japan, the trainees spent most of their time looking at the

practical side of the retail business and gaining a knowledge of com-
modities. The training in Japan fell into three broad areas:

1. *Service* — Trainees were expected to develop good customer
    services skills; to learn sales techniques; and to maintain a
    stable customer list.
2. *Merchandising* — It was hoped that trainees would develop
    a fashion sense, understand market trends, and acquire
    knowledge of purchasing, delivery, sales, stock and pricing
    control procedures. The Success Group invested heavily in the
    trainees. For example, at great expense, trainees were sent to
    attend fashion shows so that they could develop a good fashion
    sense. They were also trained to ski so as to gain knowledge
    of ski products. The Success Group expected to train them to
    be retail advisers rather than just sales professionals. A retail
    adviser should be capable of giving good advice to customers
    when selecting their purchases. Though the cost of this part of
    training was high, it produces good retail managers with expert
    knowledge.
3. *Management* — Trainees were instructed in financial manage-
    ment, personnel management, and supplies management.

Trainees were sent to different Success department stores in Japan
to gain practical experience in the above areas. In short, the training
aimed to train them as shop masters (a shop master being a person fully
responsible for the operation of a store). The training schedule had
been formulated and amended from time to time to achieve the above
goals.

Trainees started their busy, but interesting, programmes the moment
they arrived in Japan. They attended meetings with different department
store managers to understand practical operations and problems in running a store in Japan. They even learned to complete an invoice for
customers. It was also arranged that trainees should live with Japanese
families for two weeks to gain an understanding of Japanese culture.
The five months' programme was attractive to the trainees and Success
(Japan) tried hard to convert them into Japanese-minded Hong Kong
people.

At last, the trainees returned to Hong Kong. However, Success (HK) Department Store Limited did not open after seven months. Meanwhile, the trainees enthusiastically prepared for the opening and were busy contacting suppliers and collecting market information.

The Success (HK) Department Store eventually opened in 1997. Surprisingly, there were signs of depression, disappointment and confusion on the part of trainees six months after the store opened.

In Japan, the training period for potential managers is long. Large companies require them to work their way from the very bottom and move up slowly. This is the Japanese style of training.

Hence, the trainees act as retail advisers in the store every day. This seemed no different from that of a sales assistant's position in any other retail store in Hong Kong, although they were getting considerably more pay.

Before the opening of the department store in Hong Kong, Success surprisingly recruited a group of managers who had previously worked for different local department stores. The original Japanese Success culture learned by the trainees could not be put into operation at all.

Despite intensive, costly training, over 90% of the "Success executive trainees" left the organization within the first two years. In other words, the programme had failed and the HK$10 million training expenditure represented a complete loss.

Questions for Discussion

1. Why did the training programme fail?
2. Can the Success Group's corporate culture ever be successful in Hong Kong?

7

Resettlement of Locally Enlisted Personnel of the British Forces Hong Kong

Charles C. W. Man

Background

As 30 June 1997 approaches, you may think of the disappearing signs of British rule, in terms of the crown on postage stamps, the Union Jack on government buildings, etc. But there is something more tangible, prominent and important in the British administration than these — the British Forces Hong Kong. Over the past few decades, the armed forces have recruited many local Hong Kong Chinese to undertake various functions such as driving, engineering and cooking. These locally recruited members of the Forces are called locally enlisted personnel (LEP).

Before 1995, there were 1,200 LEPs in the British Forces, serving mainly in the Royal Navy (RN) and the Hong Kong Military Service Corps (HKMSC). These LEPs were usually between 21 and 49 years of age and had been serving for four to twenty-eight years in the Forces. In January 1996, 720 LEPs were still serving when the Forces planned to downsize in the following months to zero by the end of June 1997.

Table 1 shows the kind of occupations usually held by LEPs in the Forces. As in May 1996, there were 146 LEPs serving in the RN as marine engineers, cooks and mess staff. Meanwhile, 113 and 112 LEPs served in the HKMSC as drivers and guards respectively.

The Resettlement Team

Capt. Philip Lee, Resettlement Officer, said that LEPs' daily jobs were

Table 1: Ten Most Frequent Occupations of the LEPs in the HKMSC

Post	No.
Driver	113
Guard	112
Guard dog handler	52
Store keeper	30
Clerk	20
General duties	16
Medical technician	15
Cook	14
Intelligence/Security	13
Telecommunication technician	13

comparable to those in the civilian world, but the personnel also had some extra strengths that made them more competitive than others, such as loyalty, self-motivation, flexibility, maturity, to name just a few.

Capt. Lee also cited two examples to demonstrate his claim: ex-warrant officers Michael Choi and Jimmy Kong in the official promotional folder. After finishing their military service, Michael Choi acts as the security officer in the Hong Kong University of Science and Technology (HKUST) and Jimmy Kong as the transportation coordinating officer in the Airport Authority Hong Kong.

Figure 1 shows the flow of communication and responsibility of the LEPs' resettlement structure in Hong Kong. On the top is the Commander of the British Forces (CBF) (Maj. Gen. B. H. Dutton), who controls all matters relating to the resettlement staff and LEPs in both the RN and HKMSC. The resettlement centre is led by the Chief Education & Training Services Officer (Lt. Col. John Justin), the Group Education Officer (Maj. David Gibb), a senior resettlement officer (Capt. Albert Lam), a resettlement officer (Capt. Philip Lee) and two warrant officers. And all LEPs are directly under the leading of the Commanding Officer (CO HMS Tamar) and Inspector of HKMSC.

Capt. Albert Lam, Senior Resettlement Officer, said the resettlement plan has to be carried out with three conditions kept in mind: operational requirements, budget, and available training expertise and

Figure 1: Responsibility for Resettlement Provision

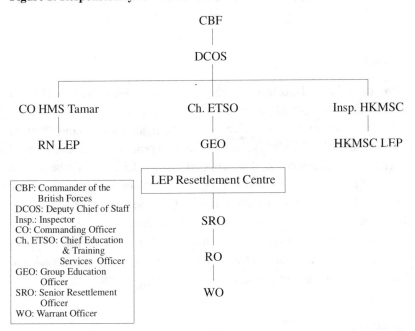

resources. It faces, therefore, two needs: a mission statement, and a plan of action.

As the British Forces comprises a highly disciplined military organization, morale, discipline, loyalty and efficiency all play an important role. Capt. Lee has to maintain the LEPs' morale and motivation and work efficiency at a peak until their last day in the Forces. It is one of the prime responsibilities of the resettlement centre "to prepare and train all LEPs as thoroughly as possible to enable each individual LEP to gain employment immediately after discharge at the highest level he or she can attain." As a consequence, the British Forces have provided a wide range of resettlement and retraining activities for LEPs in the hope that they can get new jobs before leaving the Forces.

Two Phases to Remedy the Problems

According to Capt. Lam, the LEP resettlement programme is divided into two main phases (see Figure 2), comprising four major aspects: counselling, retraining, re-employment and financial support.

Counselling

In the first phase (December 1995 to February 1996), the resettlement officers interviewed all LEPs individually and discussed their plans, problems and targets. The officers gave them advice to enable them to prepare themselves both psychologically and practically for the change. After this initial interview, it was hoped that the LEPs would be able to identify their transferable skills and formulate plans of action to prepare for second careers in their chosen fields. The resettlement officers were always at hand to give informal advice and encouragement.

Final interviews took place from September to November 1996, in an attempt to ensure that resettlement training was on the right track and that job placements were progressing according to plan.

Retraining

The second phase of this programme lasted from April to December 1996. During this time, LEPs were given a number of retraining and resettlement courses, e.g. Putonghua, computer literacy and property management.

The British Forces also cooperated with the Employees Retraining Board (ERB) in running a special two-day induction and job search course at Hong Kong College of Technology (HKCT). This course, sponsored and funded by ERB, included various aspects of job searching, e.g. an introduction to the current job market, writing résumés and application letters, interview techniques, interpersonal and communication skills, skills audit and stress management.

Other predominantly evening courses sponsored by ERB and held at HKCT comprised:

1. Managerial training for property management
2. Supervisory training for property management
3. Practice of import and export trade

4. Tour escort training

5. Chinese data entry method (Chang-Jie)

6. Introduction to computer and English word-processing

7. Putonghua and introduction to simplified Chinese characters

8. Introduction to establishment and management for smaller business

Meanwhile, the British Forces took care of the benefits of those LEPs who had the right of abode in the United Kingdom. A three-man team from the United Kingdom was invited to give two briefing sessions on "Living and Working in the United Kingdom" and "Job Search." About 100 LEPs with this rights attended related courses such as facilities management, health and safety management, security management, supervisory management and building maintenance. In November 1996, a self-funded briefing concerning house purchase and finance was given by a British property consultant with the aid of a solicitor and financial consultant.

In addition to the job search briefing, LEPs were given language courses in English and Putonghua, enabling them to sit for such public examinations as the University of London Graded English Test and HKCEE, as a part of upgrading their formal qualification. The Putong-hua course proved to be especially popular as Putonghua is the official language of China.

All these courses were provided on a voluntary basis, i.e. LEPs attended these courses in their own time. This was the only possibility because resources in the Forces became scarcer as the downsizing continued.

Re-employment

In addition to providing retraining courses, the resettlement team of the armed forces also held a job fair on 19 December 1996, comprising 40 companies such as security companies, property management, etc. which were interested in employing LEPs. One of the criteria in choosing the appropriate companies was that the jobs provided should not adversely affect the image of LEP as a military force.

Figure 2: Resettlement Programme of LEP

Year 1995–96	Year 1996									Year 1997		
Apr. 95–Mar. 96	Apr.	May	June	July	Aug.	Sept.	Oct.	Nov.	Dec.	Jan.	Feb.	Mar.
Resettlement Advice Briefing (Dec. 95–Feb. 96)	12–15 & 29 First aid in-service training	7 Security management Level 1 & 2	3–7 First aid in-service tranining									

Final Resettlement Board (Oct.–Dec. 1996)

Job placement (Jan.–Mar. 1997)

26 × ERB Sponsored Course: Induction course for LEPs of the British Forces (2-day full-time) — 7 June to 20 Sept.

ERB Resettlement Training Courses (Evening classes) — Sept.–Dec. 1996

In-service Training — Fire Safety

Advanced Certificate in Professional Security Management (Evening class)

Certificate in Professional Security Management (Evening class)

ERB Sponsored Evening Courses:

- Managerial training for property management
- Supervisory training for property management
- Practice of import & export trade
- Tour escort training
- Chinese data entry method (Chang-Jie)
- Introduction to computer & English word-processing
- Putonghua and introduction to simplified Chinese characters
- Introduction to establishment & management for smaller business

Jan. 96 ← → Dec. 96

2-day computing courses

Basic Putonghua

Intermediate Putonghua

U.K. Resettlement Training (British passport holders only)

Financial Support

As Capt. Lee pointed out, all LEPs were entitled to the annual education allowance for their retraining use and self-development, making them in his opinion all financially well supported by the Forces so that they needed not be bothered concerning financing for the training they wanted.

LEPs are currently offered financial assistance in three different ways:

1. An annual education allowance to support LEPs' individual education.
2. Special government-funded retraining courses for LEPs.
3. A lump-sum payment for all LEPs, comprising a gratuity for completed service and redundancy compensation.

Leaving the Army

Irrespective of what the Forces may have done to maintain the high morale and efficiency of LEPs, they all eventually have to face redundancy.

According to Table 2, by the end of March 1997, a total of 518 LEPs will be retired. The remaining 155 LEPs will retire by the end of June. Thus, together with those in Tranche 1, a total of 673 LEPs will be left redundant. In other words, 673 new workforce members will join an already depressed labour market at that time.

Criticism of the Plan

In view of the fact that still more LEPs were to become unemployed, critics say that the Forces had done *too little* and *too late* to resettle them. The critics believe that a large number of LEPs would not be re-employed before leaving the armed forces. The British Forces, however, argue that the plan is not little and not late, and explain that the local young people already knew the deadline of the British administration in Hong Kong, but a large number of them still applied to join the

Table 2: LEP Redundancy Plan, Phase 2 Redundancy Tranches 1–3

	Tranche 1	Tranche 2	Tranche 3	
Last day in post	31 Dec. 96	31 Mar. 97	30 Jun. 97	Total
Last day in service	31 Mar. 97	30 Jun. 97	30 Jun. 97	
RN	140	43	34	217
HKMSC	378	43	35	456
Total	518	86	69	673

Forces and be members of LEPs. In fact, they already had had plenty of time to consider and prepare for leaving the Forces.

Effectiveness of the Plan

During Phase 1 of the resettlement plan, some LEPs had found new jobs in such organizations as HKUST, Airport Authority, Hong Kong Telecom, etc., though, as Table 3 shows, there were many (Own businesses) registering as self-employed.

In short, the Forces claim this comprehensive resettlement package shows their commitment to LEPs.

Table 3: Top Six Categories of Job Placement from 1 April 1994 to 31 March 1995

Occupation	No.	Remarks
Own businesses	146	Trading, printing, transportation, food & beverages, etc.
Driver	67	Taxis, mini-buses, lorries, etc.
Security Mgr/Offr/Supr/Guard	38	Scattered over the security field
Emigrated	36	Canada, U.S., U.K., Singapore
Disciplinary forces	27	Police, firemen, customs & excise, correctional services
Salesmen	22	Trading, insurance, travel, food supply, retail, etc.

Capt. Lam, in a questionnaire interview, pointed out that the salaries offered by the participating companies in the 1996 job fair ranged from HK$10,000 to $25,000, and the participating companies were mostly from the transportation, hotel, security, property management and insurance industries. The salary level is lower than the current salary level of LEPs, since present salaries range from a private HK$16,000 to a major HK$50,000 per month.

Questions for Discussion

1. As a human resources professional, do you think the work experience of LEPs is very limited? If so, would you consider employing a younger person with the same or very similar experience?
2. What factors do contribute to the decrease in morale and efficiency of LEPs?
3. Comment on the idea of attending the retraining courses on a voluntary basis.
4. Do you think that the LEPs' argument against the criticisms is thin?

References

1. Applebaum, S., Simpson, R., and Shapiro B. "The Tough Test of Downsizing." In *Human Resources Management — Readings*, edited by F. K. Foulkes. New Jersey: Prentice-Hall, 1989; pp. 103–13.
2. Lam, A., Lee, P., and Thornborough, S. "Resettlement of Locally Enlisted Personnel of the British Garrison in Hong Kong" (Presentation Paper). Hong Kong: Military Service Corps, 1996.
3. LEP Resettlement Centre. "The Best Trained Workforce in Hong Kong" (Promotional Folder). Hong Kong: Hong Kong Military Service Corps, 1996.

Part IV

Management and Development

8

In Pursuit of Ideals
and Self-development

Olivia Ip

The Firm

John Law, aged twenty-six and single, is an Engineering Manager at CW Components Limited. The company, a manufacturing firm that produces electrical components, has about 600 employees in China. It is a typical Chinese family business, which was started in Hong Kong twenty years ago. The firm employed about 300 employees before it made the decision to move all production to China. The electrical components are sold in Hong Kong and exported to Japan, the United States, and other overseas markets.

John joined the firm two years ago when it started its project in Baoan, a county in the Pearl River Delta economic development zone. It is close to Hong Kong like its neighbouring county, Shenzhen, and has the added advantage of being less regulated. In fact, labour costs in Baoan are half those in the Shenzhen Special Economic Zone. It is easier to establish *guanxi* (relationships) there and the county officials are local people eager to bring foreign investment into the community.

John Law's Work

John spends most of his working hours in Baoan, where he is responsible for one of three production lines. The company has a flat organization structure and John has to take up a variety of responsibilities, including production management, the purchase of raw materials, inventory control, staff recruitment and training, and other duties. Recently, he has been assigned the task of providing technical support to sales and has had to spend some time in the company's headquarters at Tai Po, Hong Kong.

John works long and irregular hours and has a heavy travel schedule. He has to tackle the problem of untrained workers who come from different provinces and counties in China and speak different dialects. There is also the problem of a high labour turnover rate.

In spite of this, John still likes his present job for a number of reasons.

Firstly, he has seen how backward China is in the field of engineering. He is determined to help train and develop engineers there and, by so doing, raise levels of technological ability. This desire is deep-rooted because of John's overseas experience. Because of the 1997 issue, his family emigrated to Canada in the 1970s, where he finished his secondary and university education. During his time there, John never completely blended into the Canadian community and continues to have a strong affinity with Hong Kong and China. Deep down, he hopes that China can become an advanced economy and such hopes give considerable meaning to his current job.

Secondly, John thinks that his job provides good opportunities for self-development. He has actively participated in the start-up and running of Baoan project. This has been a very good learning experience for him because, in the past two years, he has dealt with and solved numerous problems. A strong sense of achievement remains a driving force.

Besides, his present boss, Chan Tai-nan, is a kind man who also shares John's ideals. There is a good working relationship between them.

The Company's Personnel Policy

Chan Tai-nan, Managing Director of CW Components Limited, runs the factory along typical family business lines. Before the expansion in China, the factory's management hierarchy consisted only of himself, his two sons, and a number of other relatives. John was recruited as a result of the expansion.

Chan considers John a competent young man who has vision. He is offering John a remuneration package in line with the market rate but knows that unless a promotion system and staff development programme are established, he will not be able to retain John for long.

Questions for Discussion

1. Do you agree with Chan that he will have difficulty in keeping John in his company? Why?
2. Review the personnel issues of CW Components Limited.
3. What recommendations would you make to the management of CW Components regarding personnel policy for executive staff engaged in China operations?

Part V

Compensation and Benefits

9

Who Is Staying?

Simon C. K. Wong

The Supreme Garment Company Limited was founded in 1989. Its main business is in trading sportswear products. Mr. Chan, the Director and founder of the company, is an energetic and hardworking manager. He is recognized as a fair and experienced boss in the garment business.

Chan started the company with only five employees but by 1992, the workforce had expanded to 100 employees. The company consists of six departments, namely Accounting and Finance (25 staff), Human Resources and Administration (10), Production (20), Quality Control (13), Shipping (20) and Merchandising (10).

Because of the open door policy of the Chinese government, many manufacturers have already moved their plants to cities in southern part of Guangdong province like Shenzhen and Dongguan. Attracted by the low cost of land and labour in China, Chan also thinks that it is better for the company to keep a closer link to manufacturers there for communication and coordination reasons. Having analysed the situation, Chan has decided to relocate the Production and Quality Control departments to China.

His plan was to set up a branch office in Guangzhou consisting of the Production (25 staff) and Quality Control (13) teams, as well as three administration and five accounts staff, i.e. a total workforce of 46 employees in Guangzhou.

Under this relocation plan, it is inevitable that some employees in the Hong Kong office will have to be made redundant. After many meetings with department heads, the management has at last compiled a "Redundancy List" which reads as follows:

1. 15 production employees including the production manager and garment technicians
2. 13 quality controllers
3. 1 human resources clerk
4. 1 administration clerk
5. 3 accounts clerks
6. 2 shipping clerks

Five garment technicians and all other employees will remain in Hong Kong which will serve at the headquarters coordinating with the external world of business with the internal production line in China.

Having made up his mind, Chan decided to launch an action plan for establishing the office in Guangzhou as well as a redundancy programme for Hong Kong-based employees. He delegated the project of setting up the Guangzhou Office to the financial controller and the redundancy programme to the human resources manager, Mr. Li.

The new office tenancy agreement in Guangzhou was signed for the period 1 November 1995 until 30 October 1997. Under this arrangement, Li had to lay off redundant staff by 31 December 1995. After several long meetings, the management finally designed an attractive package for "redundant" employees which would enable the company to retain them up until 31 December 1995. As these employees possess strong product knowledge, they would become a skeleton training team for new staff recruited in Guangzhou.

Chan and Li informed the employees involved on 20 March 1995, and gave them nine months to arrange all necessary transfers.

The terms of the redundancy package (provided employees worked until 31 December 1995) include:

1. one month's salary in lieu of notice;
2. year-end bonus (13th month salary);
3. discretionary bonus equal to one month's salary;
4. severance payments in line with the Hong Kong Employment

Ordinance: two-thirds of last month's salary (maximum ceiling: HK$15,000) × no. of years and months of service;
5. provident fund, equal to employees' contribution plus Employer's contribution portion depending on the years of service;

Completed years of service	Employer's contribution portion (%)
2	20
3	30
4	40
5	50
6	60
7	70
8	80
9	90
10 years or above	100

6. additional two months' salary as incentive bonus (provided employees work until 31 December 1995).

All employees on the redundancy list were pleased to accept the terms of this offer, especially the two months' incentive bonus. All agreed to work until 31 December 1995 and signed a redundancy agreement with the management.

Chan was very satisfied with his redundancy package. However, things began to go wrong after three months. Starting July 1995, he received many resignations from employees that were not on the redundancy list.

Li approached Chan for a serious discussion about how to handle the situation. There was a problem of finding replacements at the end of the year, so Chan proposed retaining of some of those employees who had received the "redundancy package." However, only two of them were willing to cancel the agreements and stay on. All other employees insisted on keeping the "redundancy package" because some of them had already acquired new jobs, and some would like to use the money for vacation.

The management now faced the problem of retaining employees on the "redundancy list" as well as those employees not on the list. Both groups were vital to the operation because the Guangzhou office was not yet complete.

Chan and Li decided to ask existing employees by conducting exit interviews with each of them.

To their surprise, many exit interviewees expressed resentment towards the employees on the "redundancy list." They complained that those who would be made redundant were uncooperative and reluctant to offer assistance to other colleagues. They worked to minimum standards, and were unwilling to work overtime anymore, but claimed that they were just working according to their "job descriptions."

Those on the redundancy list felt that they were "victims" of the relocation plan and were reluctant to perform well for the company. The consequence was that existing employees had to work even harder to cover the work of demotivated "redundant" employees. The existing employees felt that they were unfairly treated because those on the redundancy list had received a very attractive package to "protect" their jobs, while existing employees were given no incentives at all. They thought the company was bias in offering an attractive package to "redundant" staff at the expense of the existing employees.

Morale of existing and "redundant" employees was low. The former believed themselves to be unfairly treated and, therefore, is going to leave without regret once another job is available. The latter has to leave after 31 December 1995 and, therefore, works from 9:00 a.m. to 6:00 p.m. without initiatives and just according to the job descriptions.

Chan and Li faced a dilemma as to whether they should offer an incentive to existing employees, or apply disciplinary measures to future "redundant employees" whom they were relying upon during the critical period leading up to the opening of the Guangzhou office.

Questions for Discussion

1. What do you think of the way in which employees behaved in this case?
2. How would you react to the redundancy deal if you were:
   a. a member of the redundancy group?

    b. a member of the remaining group?

3. If you believe the situation was not managed effectively, what improvements would you suggest at this stage?

10

Good Taste Foods Limited

C. Lok

The Company

Good Taste Foods Limited is a public company which manufactures and distributes a variety of snack foods, including candies, potato chips, crackers, and bakery items. It is the leading manufacturer in the industry with its head office in Aberdeen and two manufacturing plants in Hong Kong and Shenzhen, the two regional offices which handle sales in Hong Kong and other regions in China respectively.

The Industry

The snack food industry is very tactical in nature, i.e. daily operating decisions regarding pricing, distribution and manufacturing often have a significant impact on both sales and profitability. The industry is also very competitive, and its excess capacity has often led to significant price reductions, as many of the smaller manufacturers have to sell their products just above cost to keep operations running.

Company Operations

Most of Good Taste's daily operating decisions are made in the Hong Kong head office by a management team, comprising a President and five Vice Presidents (for sales, marketing, manufacturing, human resources and finance). The decisions made at head office include major retail advertising initiatives, pricing, product line additions and capital expenditure. The two regional offices have some control over retail discounts, non-advertised promotions, warehousing and daily productions. However, for the most part, regional managers are expected to carry out the decisions made by head office.

For years now, regional managers have expressed their frustration at their lack of autonomy. They have questioned the underlying rationale of head office decisions, claiming that senior management does not recognize their unique operating environments. The regional managers explain that corporate policies impair their ability to compete with some of the innovative programmes offered by their regional competitors. In addition, the head office decision-making process is becoming increasingly inefficient as the business becomes more complex. Recently, several last-minute promotional opportunities were missed because Good Taste was unable to respond to the retailers rapidly enough.

Performance bonus

Company targets for sales, market share, profitability and return on shareholders' equity are established in the annual operating plan. The members of the senior management team are eligible for lucrative bonuses if these targets are reached. The bonuses comprise cash, stock options and additional perks, such as paid vacations.

Through the corporate sales plan, the Vice President of Sales establishes gross sales and market share objectives for each of the two regional sales managers. A cash bonus of 20% of base salary is available to each regional sales manager who attains both objectives. The bonus scale is set so that the reward diminishes rapidly if either sales or market share falls even slightly below target.

The Vice President of Manufacturing establishes targets for the production managers. The production managers receive a bonus based on the average cost per kilogram produced and the quality of the finished product. An average annual quality index is used to gauge plant quality. This is determined by independent audits throughout the year from Good Taste's head office using criteria such as taste, colour and seasoning application. The bonus scale for production managers is similar to that used for the regional sales managers.

Financial Results

The end of the financial year is now approaching and senior management is in the process of reviewing the financial results for the first six months. Overall sales have continued to decline and profits are well below budget. Furthermore, retail discounts, freight costs, warehousing and the cost of goods sold are well above targeted levels.

The corporate Vice President of Finance, May Chan, presenting the details of the financial results to the President during the staff meeting, states that each of the two regions, especially the Hong Kong market, is performing below target. May asks the members of the senior management team why the results are so poor across the two operating regions.

As no conclusion is reached in the meeting, the senior management resolves to contract Henry Chan, a management consultant, to examine the performance bonus system in the company.

Henry's first task is to examine the situation in Hong Kong.

Hong Kong makes up about 50% of Good Taste's sales and profits. Hong Kong has been severely affected by the economic downturn and a high rate of unemployment. Johnny Wong, the Hong Kong sales manager, blames stiff competition in the Hong Kong market for the poor interim financial results. He points out that deep price cutting has been necessary to achieve the gross sales and market share objectives, and adds that recent product supply shortages have resulted in several missed sales opportunities. If product supply issues persist, Johnny fears that the sales force will react with higher absenteeism resulting in higher selling costs.

The Hong Kong Production Manager, Kelvin Chow, is outraged at Johnny's accusation of his plant's poor product supply. He explains that last-minute sales promotions and order changes have caused higher costs in the plant. In addition, Kelvin complains about the number of product line items his plant must produce, stating that this is causing increases in costs and down time.

Question for Discussion

As Henry Chan, identify the performance bonus issues facing the Hong Kong office of Good Taste and make appropriate recommendations.

11

Rewarding and Promoting
the Right Employees

Theresa Lau

"It's 7 p.m. already, I'd better get some work done." As Peter Louis thought to himself, he sat down at his desk and took out his work folder. It had been a long day for him as he had been interviewing a number of staff and listening to their complaints. After which, he had a long discussion with his boss when he sought to work out a solution to those complaints.

Peter Louis was not the Personnel Manager though he always seemed to be involved in handling personnel problems. Peter was the General Manager of the Laboratory Testing Division of a leading testing laboratory company in Hong Kong. He held a B.Sc. degree in chemistry and had been working in the company for four years. The organization structure of the company follows a simple and rather traditional framework that is reproduced in Figure 1. The company used to enjoy a leading position in the industry. However, a number of new competitors having recently entered the testing market posed a threat to its position in the 1990s. In order to maintain a competitive edge, Mr. Stevenson, the Managing Director, accepted the recommendations made by a consultant and attempted to restructure the company from a client basis to a functional basis. The new structure, with changes in the Textile Testing Department, is presented in Figure 2. As a result of the organizational changes, overall efficiency has increased by 20%, and morale has been enhanced. So, it came as a surprise for him this morning to hear that four members of staff in this department might resign: namely, Mr. So, the

Figure 1: Organization Structure before Restructuring

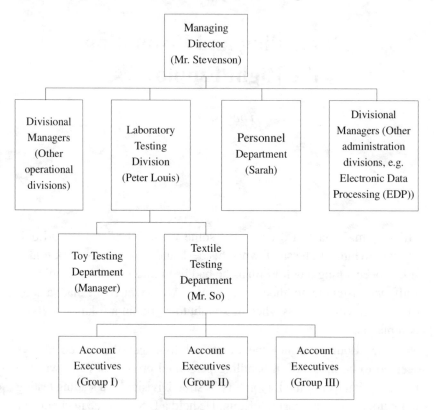

Department Manager and three operators under him, i.e. Alex, Betty and Connie.

Upon receiving the resignation letters, Peter talked to each of the four staff members to find out their reasons for quitting. He discovered that the operators had been upset by the promotion decision made by Mr. Stevenson. Working in the Textile Testing Department as operators was an extremely boring job since it required high concentration and repetitive work. For instance, they might spend the whole day doing cloth washing, cloth rubbing or cloth ironing. As a consequence of the dull nature of the work, turnover had always been particularly high in this department.

It was the company's policy to conduct an annual salary review

Figure 2: Organization Structure after Restructuring

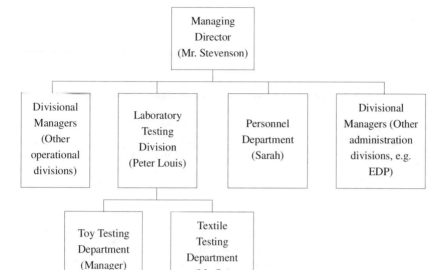

and promotion exercise in December every year, but in July of every year, the company established an unwritten practice of repeating the same exercise. Mr. So, the Department Manager, promised to promote Alex and Betty two months ago. He expressed this view verbally to Peter so that recommendations could be made in the July review and submitted to the Managing Director (see attached note written by Peter Louis in Table 1). In addition, Mr. So also recommended promoting Connie provided that her performance improved over the next few months. Mr. Stevenson received the report from Peter sometime in June and passed it to Sarah, the Personnel Manager, for consideration. Sarah, however, had a different view. She wanted to promote Connie but not the other two. When she passed the recommendation to Mr. Stevenson

Table 1: Peter's Note to the Managing Director

To: T. H. Stevenson
From: Peter Louis

The following salary adjustments are proposed with effect from 1st July.

Dept.	Name	Service	Grade	Present salary	Range for Grade	Proposed Salary	Justification
				$	$	$	
Textile Testing	Alex	3 years	Technician	15,200	14,500–15,600	15,600	Promotion to Senior Technician
	Betty	3 years	Technician	15,000	14,500–15,600	15,400	Promotion to Senior Technician
	*Connie	4 years	Senior Technician	16,200	15,400–17,200	16,700	Promotion to Laboratory Executive

* Very competent but somewhat not motivated enough; promotion might be effective
  after a few months' observation of her performance.

for approval, the latter was hesitant in making any decision. It seemed that he was not happy with the idea of promoting any employees, due to the unsatisfactory financial situation in that year. Additionally, the July review was not seen by him to be essential.

When Mr. So heard about the decision in the morning, he was very upset. He came to see Peter and said that he did not feel like working in the company anymore since, as a department head, he did not even have the authority to decide on whom he should promote under him. He reckoned that he knew his staff best and Alex and Betty really deserved to have a raise because they were the best performers and worked especially hard after the restructuring two months ago. Moreover, it was not difficult for them to find a job elsewhere, even with better pay. Therefore, in order to build up a good morale in the department, he promised to promote them in the July review. To go back in his words, not only would he lose face and credibility, but that morale in the department would drop as well. It took Peter quite a while to talk Mr. So out of his threat to resign which he did by promising that he would talk to the Managing Director about the review.

When Mr. So left his office, Peter went to the Personnel Department and asked Sarah to explain why she favoured promotion for Connie, but not Alex and Betty. Sarah maintained that Connie did not turn in her best performance because she was upset by not being promoted at the previous salary and promotion review last December. Sarah considered that the said review was not fair and Connie should be promoted this time since she was a good worker and had been with the company for a longer time. Her unsatisfactory performance immediately after the review revealed her lack of faith in the company. As a result, to promote Connie this time would motivate her to work hard again and restore her faith in the company. As for Alex and Betty, they were still new in the company and there were doubts about their loyalty to the company.

Peter then went to see Mr. Stevenson to review the whole situation. After hearing Peter's views about the impact of this decision on staff's morale, Mr. Stevenson realized the predicament and considered both Mr. So and Sarah had a point. As he did not want to appear to favour either side, he came up with an idea. He resolved to give a special bonus to some of the staff in the Textile Testing Department, in order to show management's recognition of their hard work after the restructuring. In addition, since this was the department that had had the highest increase in output since then, the bonus would help to keep up current performance levels. As for the July review, it was not considered necessary and he did not see the point of promoting anyone or offering a raise in salary. The raise could be delayed to December.

When Peter conveyed Mr. Stevenson's decision to Sarah and Mr. So, they had another difference of opinion as to whom the special bonus should be given. Should it be given to the staff of the whole department or only the better performers? Finally, they agreed upon a list, which included the three operators who eventually agreed to stay in the company.

Peter heaved a sigh of relief as he came back to his office at 7 p.m. and started his routine work for the day again. While he was working, he thought: "That's settled this time, but what will happen at the next salary and promotion review in December?"

Questions for Discussion

1. Comment on the company's staff rewarding methods. What are the pros and cons of each method, and under what circumstances should they be used?
2. Should Sarah, the Personnel Manager, be involved in the process of rewarding staff? Why and why not? What role should the Personnel Manager play in this case?
3. Is there anything wrong with the salary review and promotion procedure in the company?

Part VI

Employee Management

12

Empowerment: We Don't Want It!

Brian Brewer and Kathryn Somers

The Palace Hotel is a five-star hotel in Hong Kong, which was established by the "C" family. As one of the family's numerous business interests, the hotel had been under the management of the "C" family for the past twenty years. A year ago, upon the death of the patriarch of the family, the family sold the hotel.

The decision to sell the hotel was made after considerable discussion and disagreement among the family members. Some were well satisfied with the hotel's fine reputation and continued profitability. Others favoured a complete refurbishment of the Palace with added features such as an upgraded business centre, in-house facsimile machines and an executive health centre. This disagreement within the family was finally resolved when a decision was made to sell the hotel to a U.S.-based international hotel chain which was interested in expansion into Asia.

Currently, the Palace Hotel has 700 employees. The General Manager, who was also a member of the "C" family, chose to retire when the hotel changed hands. The remaining management staff have remained in office and mostly worked in their previous capacities. They are Hong Kong Chinese who have worked their way up through the ranks, gaining promotions on the basis of their technical skills, seniority and loyalty to the hotel. The two exceptions are the Food & Beverage Manager and the Pastry Chef, both of whom are Swiss.

When the sale was announced, the "C" family offered 50% of the hotel's staff the possibility of relocating to one of the family's other businesses. Forty per cent elected to remain with the hotel. The resulting combination of staff can be seen to be roughly divided into two segments. There are the long-serving staff, many of whom have been with the hotel since its opening. They occupy most of the managerial positions in the hotel; there is also a group of younger front-line staff who tend to come and go quickly, their mobility being sped up by the need for their skills in the labour market.

The employees of the hotel had generally experienced a high level of job satisfaction in the past. The hotel had been a prestigious hotel in Hong Kong and many of the long-serving employees had enjoyed the status attached to working for the Palace. There were tangible benefits as well. Every Chinese New Year a bonus amounting to two to three months' salary was given to each employee regardless of the hotel's overall level of profitability during the past year.

When the American hotel chain assumed control of the Palace, they assigned Tony Brown from the United States to be the General Manager. He was chosen on the basis of his previous performance in successfully incorporating a family-run hotel, similar in size to the Palace, into the company's chain in Denver, Colorado.

The Denver hotel had been unprofitable and overstaffed. Once in charge, Tony moved quickly to implement fundamental changes. Family members left the hotel and they were not replaced. Incompetent employees or those having values not consistent with those of the chain were ousted from their positions. Department heads and managers were involved more in the decision-making processes and made responsible and accountable for running their own operations. This included handling their own budgets.

Front-line staff were encouraged to be responsive to customer needs and to rely on their own judgement within a framework with a few important set standards. Tony brought in management trainers to work with managers on decision making and empowerment-based leadership programmes and to assist in the development of service skills for front-liners.

Tony's efforts had been rewarded with considerable success. The Denver hotel began to make a profit and became known as a good place to work. The enthusiasm of the staff frequently won the praise of hotel guests.

The General Manager's position at the Palace was Tony's first overseas assignment. He was very excited about the opportunity to work in Hong Kong. He wanted to replicate his previous success in the United States. In fact, this was the expectation of the hotel chain's headquarters on him.

The first major decision that Tony made, upon his arrival, was not to replace as far as possible the 10% of the staff who had left when the hotel was sold. He believed that the hotel was overstaffed and that it was necessary to flatten the hotel's hierarchy. In line with his ideas about empowerment, he wanted the remaining managers to expand their scope of control and to take on more decision-making responsibilities. He also began a major refurbishment programme aimed at providing business travellers with facilities likewise done by many Hong Kong hotels.

The decision of not filling vacancies caused a considerable amount of dissatisfaction among the hotel's employees. This was generally perceived as a "laying off" exercise designed only to ensure an increased flow of profits back to corporate headquarters in the United States.

Managers at the Palace adhered more to tradition and loyalty rather than innovation and risk. They had always worked according to the senior management's instruction and their responsibility was to follow through instructions in a diligent and conscientious manner. Innovation was not discouraged; on the contrary, it had been the practice of the "C" family to invite hotel managers to contribute suggestions for change. However, there was an implicit understanding that only ideas with a very great chance of success were ever proposed. Mistakes were not easily forgiven!

Administrative Control had always been considered essential in the Palace. As a result, numerous bureaucratic procedures existed at every level. For example, when the front desk staff wished to upgrade any guest for another category of room, it was necessary for them to secure the approval of the Front Office Manager and make a follow-up written report. Every week a written report on the upgrades, including justifications for all actions taken, had to be submitted to the General Manager.

In order to reduce the amount of red tape, Tony began an exercise to redesign procedures and to place much more decision-making authority in the hands of individual managers and employees. He stressed the need to be flexible and responsive to customer needs. Policies were to be regarded as guidelines, subject to interpretation in light of different sets of circumstances. They were not, as he was fond of saying, "commandments written on tablets of stone."

Staff empowerment was what Tony believed in and wanted. He hired the same management trainers as he had used in the Denver operation to deliver the same programme to the Hong Kong staff.

However, the empowerment process did not proceed smoothly. Tony observed that the managers were generally reluctant to make decisions which involved "personal" risk. He understood that this was a reaction to their previous experiences when the "C" family had been in charge. Old Mr. "C" would quickly bring about the downfall of any managers who had been so foolish as to make a mistake.

Besides, the employees could not see any benefits of changing the existing system. The hotel was prospering. With China's open door policy now firmly in place, there was every reason to believe that the volume of business travellers coming to Hong Kong would continue to increase.

Fourteen months after assuming his post at the Palace, Tony met with George Sanders, the hotel chain's newly appointed Vice President for the Asia-Pacific region. The chain was beginning to consider seriously the idea of expanding into China. The new Vice President was visiting the region to get more information.

Tony had intended to present a very positive picture of developments at the Palace. However, under George's gentle but persuasive questioning, Tony began to discuss his problems at the Palace and the frustration he experienced.

"I don't understand it, George. People here just will not take responsibility for their actions. They expect top management to make all the decisions. I really can't understand it!"

"Yes, I can appreciate your frustration Tony, but any group of employees takes time to adapt to a new managerial style and I expect that things are moving along more quickly than you might think."

"Well," replied Tony, "I wish that was the case. However, if I'm honest with myself — and you — I cannot see a change for the better in this place. The staff just will not make decisions. They do not want empowerment. I have never seen anything like this before."

"I'm sorry to hear that you are feeling so discouraged," George said.

"In fact I have prepared my resignation letter. I feel I'm not the person for the job. I can't work effectively in Hong Kong. I really want to go back to the States."

"Surely not!" exclaimed George.

"Yes, I'm afraid so. I don't see any alternative. I've been totally unsuccessful in Hong Kong. I'm clearly not suited for this place."

George was shocked by Tony's revelation and expressed his dismay to an old friend over dinner that evening. His friend was a Hong Kong Chinese who had been in college with George in the United States and was now a senior executive with an American bank in Hong Kong. He nodded sympathetically as George told him about Tony's dilemma at the Palace Hotel and, after some reflection, he began his reply: "There are a few things which you need to understand ..."

Questions for Discussion

1. What do George and Tony need to understand about doing business in Hong Kong?
2. How could the changing process at the Palace Hotel in Hong Kong be managed so as to enhance the possibility of a successful outcome?

13

But It Worked Before: A Case of an Expatriate Supervisor in Hong Kong

Brian Brewer and Kathryn Somers

Ted was employed as the Ground Services Manager for Hong Kong Dragonfly Airlines in Los Angeles (LA). His managerial philosophy was consistent with empowerment. For example, the airline had a series of guidelines about the excess baggage. Ted expected employees to adhere to this principle, yet consider customer needs on a case-by-case basis. They were to consider the outcome, i.e. customer satisfaction, rather than be bound by rules. Front-line staff had the authority to waive charges without reference to supervisors and were expected to deal with problem situations independently, in cases like agitated customers. Ted encouraged staff to be customer-oriented at all times and he regularly provided positive feedback.

Inevitably, mistakes occurred from time to time. Ted made a point of discussing these with the staff concerned. Even in a situation where a customer had complained, Ted's stance was not to blame the staff but to assist them to learn through experience. In line with his expectation that staff should develop their decision-making ability, Ted could not tolerate minor decisions being brought to him for resolution.

The LA operation was characterized by a high degree of commitment from the staff, who were generally satisfied with their work environment and responded well to Ted's managerial style. Ted socialized with the staff on a fairly regular basis. Turnover of Ground Services staff at Dragonfly was lower than the industry average.

In Hong Kong, Dragonfly was being faced with a unique set of circumstances. Several new airlines had entered the industry just as an economic downturn was reducing overall demand. Aside from stiffer competition, Dragonfly's Hong Kong operation had to cope with the loss of senior staff due to emigration factor.

Given modest price differentials between airlines, discriminating travellers, particularly those in business and first-class, were becoming even more conscious of service quality. To cope with increasing competition and higher customer expectations, Dragonfly's Hong Kong operation had decided it must develop a more customer-oriented service.

In January 1997, Ted accepted a transfer from the United States to Hong Kong. Because of his excellent track record, he was considered to be an ideal person to bring Dragonfly's Hong Kong operation up to the standards which had been previously achieved in the United States. Ted assumed responsibility for managing a workforce of 120 staff who was under the supervision of ten supervisors.

Ted's task was to develop the ground check-in staff to a level where autonomous decision-making would replace dependence on supervisory direction. Supervisors were to redefine their roles in terms of "coaching" rather than "policing." Ultimately, Dragonfly wanted to reduce the number of supervisors, while offering an improved service which is more customer-oriented.

Upon taking up his post in Hong Kong, Ted arranged for a meeting of all Dragonfly ground supervisors to explain his "tough but fair" philosophy. He intended to implement exactly the same approach which had worked so successfully in the United States. Staff were to be given permission to use their own initiative for problems related to "excess baggage," "tickets with restriction" and "overbooking." More complex decisions were to be referred to the supervisors, but they were to coach and assist rather than just direct. Mistakes would be allowed, but not the same mistakes twice. Ted explained he did not expect supervisors to consult with him about minor decisions, though "his door was always open" for important issues which required quick action.

After Ted had explained his plans for implementing the new customer-oriented approach at Dragonfly, he asked the supervisors for their feedback. Several of the more vocal supervisors expressed support for Ted's ideas; the others remained silent. Ted was not surprised at the subdued response as he had heard that people in the Orient tended to be more low-key than those in the United States.

Ted established a high profile around the check-in area with a "management by wandering around" approach. In monitoring staff Ted found that he was at a disadvantageous position because he did not understand Cantonese and therefore was not always certain of what staff were saying either to customers or among themselves.

Ted was an industrious worker, putting in long hours. He was conscious of not spending much time with his wife, who had given up her executive position in an LA bank in order to accompany Ted to Hong Kong.

Ted's approach seemed to have been taken to heart by both the staff and the supervisors. However, staff have experienced some difficulty in discriminating between major and minor decisions. Their confidence was undermined when supervisors would override their decisions, sometimes even rebuking them in front of customers.

When the supervisors came to see him, Ted reiterated his principle that they should make their own decisions and sent them back to their work environment. It was consistent with his coaching philosophy and he believed it was the best way for staff to develop and to build up their own confidence.

Ted found the supervisors were consulting with him more frequently. His time was being wasted by their bombarding questions. He began to close his office door more often to attend to paperwork and make phone calls, as he discovered that when the door was closed the supervisors stayed away.

Contrary to what had been expected, the ground service at Dragonfly began to deteriorate rather than improve. Customer complaints increased. Staff became more and more reluctant to make decisions and consequently became more dependent on their supervisors. No one seemed to be earning from experience. Ted was particularly upset about having to reply to a "Letters to the Editor" in an English newspaper after an overseas traveller complained about the airline's poor service in relation to an incident at the check-in section.

Stress levels among the staff were increasing. Absenteeism due to illnesses was increasing and staff turnover was going up over the previous year. Working relationships were not as good as they had been, with a tendency for "fault picking" to take place when a mistake was made. Ted noted that the supervisors still preferred to "police" staff rather than "coach" them to develop confidence in using their own initiative.

One year after taking on his new assignment, Ted was feeling exhausted. The more customer-oriented service was not working as intended and the plans to downsize the number of supervisory staff through redeployment, etc. could not be carried out. The Hong Kong Dragonfly Company's profit was going down over the previous year and improvements in the airline's competitive position had not taken place. Ted had applied for a reassignment back to the United States.

Questions for Discussion

1. What went wrong with Ted's assignment in Hong Kong?
2. What assumptions did Ted bring to Hong Kong in human resources management?
3. Why did Ted's empowerment concept fail in Hong Kong?
4. How should Ted implement his empowerment plan in Hong Kong?

14

Euro-Coast Apparel Limited: A Case Study in Delegation

Frank Ng

Euro-Coast Apparel Limited (ECAL) is a well-established subsidiary of a large trading group in Hong Kong. It is engaged in the sourcing of lingerie for export to Europe.

Led by the Managing Director, John Kent, sales activities of the company are performed both in Hong Kong and through a branch office in Holland. This is mainly under the control of a resident Dutch Sales Director.

The Head Office in Hong Kong acts principally as an administration centre. It controls the sourcing of apparel from Southeast Asian countries, and provides merchandising and documentation services for the entire company. As a substantial amount of apparel is purchased from off-shore suppliers, John Kent and the Buying Director are out of Hong Kong for at least nine months of the year. The administration of the Hong Kong office is entirely delegated to Wallace Fu, the newly promoted Executive Director, who has worked for this company for over ten years. He oversees four Merchandising Departments and the Secretarial Department. The Shipping and Accounting Departments are centralized and under the direct control of ECAL's parent company.

Each Merchandising Department is headed by a Department Manager backed up by four Merchandising Clerks and a Sample Supervisor. The functions of these Merchandising Departments include: following up and communicating with the European branch office; liaising with clients and suppliers on orders and shipments; monitoring samples preparation from local and off-shore suppliers for dispatch to overseas clients; and processing purchase and sales documentation.

Over the past two years, the company has experienced huge staff turnover in the Merchandising Departments. Out of the twenty Merchandising Clerks, only three have been with this company for over a year. On average, two staff leave the Merchandising Departments every month although the company can easily recruit replacements through an employment agency. Such frequent changes at the operating level have damaged morale among Merchandising Clerks. As a result there has been an increase in the number of complaints from the European branch office and clients. There have also been delays in following up faxes and mistakes in the delivery of samples which have jeopardized the confidence of clients. It is becoming evident that interdepartmental cooperation is rather loose.

A meeting with the Merchandising Managers was held with the aim of addressing the problems created by the high staff turnover rate. The meeting was attended by John Kent, Wallace Fu, the Executive Secretary Ivy Lam, and the Financial Manager from the parent company.

"I think we should increase the salary of the Merchandising Clerks by putting it slightly above the market rate. Junior staff are now more concerned about money than anything else. I believe our current salaries are the main reason for high staff turnover," said Wallace Fu.

When asked by Kent to comment, the Financial Manager added, "The salary scale of Merchandising Clerks in ECAL is at the mid-level of the market range. However, our merchandising staff are entitled to receive a year-end bonus, worth two months' salary, plus commission sharing worth approximately one and a half months' salary. This is in line with the remuneration of other Group companies' for junior staff."

The Executive Secretary added that junior staff were now more demanding. She suggested that there should be changes in the rigid system that separated staff job duties such as typing, data inputting and sample checking. She also asked whether rotation of job duties or staff re-grading could be considered, as these might improve departmental cohesiveness and coordination.

"I think we are already facing serious workload problems on daily clerical routines. Rotation, or changes of staff duties, would interrupt our tight schedules. I suggest each Department should take a flexible approach to solving its work and staff problems," said one of the Merchandising Managers. The other Merchandising Managers quickly supported this view.

After much argument on this issue, there was no agreement by the end of the meeting. A compromise was reached where each Department Manager was allowed to adopt flexible tactics to tackle his own department's problems. John Kent delegated the entire matter to Wallace Fu. He asked him to liaise with the Merchandising Managers of other Group companies and to submit a proposal for reducing staff turnover. The overall aim should be to improve the operational efficiency of the Merchandising Departments of ECAL.

In June, the Executive Director informed the Board that he was resigning from his position in ECAL because he was emigrating to Canada in three months. Privately, he told John Kent that he did not have any solid proposal for improving the existing merchandising staff structure.

Shortly after this news, Kent also learnt that two Merchandising Managers had successfully obtained visas to emigrate to Canada. One of them would leave the company in three months, the other in six months.

Shocked by the impending change in senior management personnel, Kent began to worry. There appeared to be no staff in the company to fill these vacancies. The experience and qualifications of Merchandising Assistants within the Departments were inadequate. He also doubted whether he had adopted the right management style in delegating complete authority to his staff in office administration.

The Hong Kong brain drain was hitting his company very hard.

Questions for Discussion

1. What management style did John Kent adopt?
2. Do you consider that the Executive Secretary's suggestion of changes in the job specifications of merchandising staff would have improved department cohesiveness and operational efficiency?

3. What changes should be made to the organizational structure of the company to reduce staff turnover, and cushion the brain drain problem?

15

Getting People to Do Their Best

Judy Ng

Background

Teresa Ho has just been appointed as the first Human Resources Manager of a newly established Japanese subsidiary company in Hong Kong. The company, Konichiwa Precision Inc. (KPI), manufactures aluminium substrates, the core material in computer memory disks.

As a manager of human resources, she has to encounter a wide variety of people both inside and outside the company. Her major task is to establish some basic programmes to enhance organizational communication.

Teresa is responsible for directing the planning, development, implementation, administration, and budgeting of all personnel programmes. This includes recruitment and selection, compensation, employee benefits, employee relations, affirmative action, and management training and development.

Local labour culture, particularly the working habits of the Hong Kong Chinese, is perplexing to her Japanese colleagues. She believes that good communications, time, and patience will result in fewer misunderstandings in the future.

The Human Resources Programmes at KPI

Since KPI is new to Hong Kong, Teresa's first task involves designing and establishing some basic human resources programmes. She believes that maintaining a healthy working environment is essential for employee satisfaction. Here are some of the programmes that she believes will help her achieve this.

The Initial Progress Report

Teresa would like to begin by establishing an Initial Progress Report (IPR) system. It is designed for new employees who have been with the company for sixty days, the usual probationary period. During this period, new employees get acquainted with the company and their responsibilities. Three weeks before the end of this period, an IPR is sent to the new recruit's direct supervisor. The supervisor completes this document and formally meets with the new employee to review his/her progress, outline the areas of improvement, and decide whether further training is needed over the next three months. In this report, the supervisor also has to decide whether the employee is suitable for the post and then recommend whether the appointment be confirmed.

This is an opportunity for the employee to ask specific questions and express any concerns. As this document is concerned with the employee's performance, it must be signed by both parties and placed in the employee's personnel file.

The New Employee Survey

A second priority is the implementation of a New Employee Survey (NES). This is given to employees who have worked for a minimum of ninety days, that is, thirty days after satisfactory completion of the probationary period. This document supplements the IPR and focuses on factors related to KPI more generally. The survey allows new employees to express their views or concerns about the quality of training, the equipment they are responsible for, benefits, and the company's policies and procedures.

"The key here is to act upon these answers in a positive way to encourage and build employees' trust in management," says Teresa.

The information collected by this survey is kept private and does not need to be reviewed by a supervisor. The Human Resources Department shares the results with management and makes adjustments that would improve internal communications.

The Suggestion Programme

Teresa believes that two-way communications between employee and management are necessary. Thus, the Suggestion Programme (SP) is modelled after the parent company's programme. The main objective is to get employees involved, either collectively or individually, in making their jobs more challenging such that there is an impact on cost-savings, quality, safety and productivity. Those employees whose suggestions are implemented are rewarded whereas rejected suggestions are returned to employees without any explanation.

In order to promote this programme, Teresa will launch a new theme — "Keep Producing Ideas" — a slogan that plays on the acronym of the company's name. Posters and badges remind employees that they and their ideas count.

"It's fun and healthy to have these themes incorporated into active programmes to promote participation and variation," say Teresa.

A memo will also be sent to supervisors that will clearly define objectives and require them to actively incorporate the use of the SP as part of their job responsibilities.

Questions for Discussion

Management Questions

1. All managers need technical, human and conceptual skills in carrying out their work. What do these skills involve? In which of the three managerial skills do you think Teresa Ho should be stronger?
2. Managers perform the four basic managerial functions of planning, organizing, directing/influencing, and controlling. For this case, do you think Teresa Ho has carried out these functions?

Human Resource Questions

1. If you were Teresa Ho, what criteria would you include in the Initial

Progress Report that would help you to evaluate an employee's progress in the organization during their probationary period?

2. The purpose of the New Employee Survey questionnaire is to provide a means of recording the observations of new employees during their induction into KPI. Write down *at least five* questions to be included in this questionnaire if this purpose is to be achieved.

3. In the Suggestion Programme, give *at least two* examples of suggestions that would fall under the activity of:
   a. cost reduction,
   b. product development,
   c. safety,
   d. convenience.

16

The Red Pot's Dismissal

R. Lee and C. Lok

"Go to the Ocean Hotel. Go to the Red Pot Restaurant" had long been a popular slogan in town. Throughout its six years' operation, the Red Pot Restaurant had frequently been mentioned in newspapers and on television. It had 100 seats and served a wide range of delicious Thai Seafood dishes and other Thai delicacies, including satays, coconut-based deserts, curry crabs and dim-sum. Its food was mouth-watering for new and old customers alike. Tourists and local customers never missed the chance of taking close-up photographs of the large red pot standing in the doorway, the symbol of the Red Pot Restaurant. The restaurant itself was one of the six Ocean Hotel outlets. Customers were able to sample the dishes served to them by the friendly warm-hearted staff, as they sat in full view of the harbour listened to soft Thai music, played by the hotel band. It was regarded as the busiest outlet in the hotel and had frequently topped the sales record throughout the years.

Nevertheless its name had gradually lost much of its glamour since 1997, setting off alarm bells in the Food and Beverage Department and among the top management of the hotel. They saw the customers dwindle and faced a 100% staff turnover. Newly recruited staff resigned soon before finishing the probation period and the casual helpers who were employed to help out were totally inexperienced in handling customers. Anyone entering the outlet felt the tense atmosphere inside. The former sunny faces of the staff in the past were now replaced by expressions of gloom.

The top management and the Food and Beverage Director had monitored the situation with anxiety. At first they attributed the phenomenon to an increasing workload and staff laxness after years of service. They tried looking into the matter from every aspect and interviewed the various levels of staff carefully. They found that at first the staff were unwilling to disclose anything but after much persuasion and roundabout questioning, they discovered that they all criticized the managerial style and unfairness of their new Restaurant Manager, Mr. Mark Lee.

Mark had been employed by the hotel since its opening as bar captain and then Assistant Bar Manager. Prior to joining the hotel chain, he had been in the hotel industry for four years. Ever since he joined the Ocean Hotel, he had worked hard and scored very high with regard to all the items in the employment record, namely hospitality, knowledge of the trade, practicality and attentiveness, etc. Furthermore, he worked well with his colleagues and the outlet he served often obtained the best sales results. He had been named the most outstanding manager of the year two times. Finally, his chance came and Mark, who secretly thought of promotion in the near future, found his dreams come time with the retirement of old John, the Red Pot Restaurant Manager.

The top management cautiously pondered the idea of promoting Mark, but they also considered transferring a restaurant manager from another outlet which served Chiu Chow dishes in the hotel. Finally, they however, decided to give Mark a chance after considering his outstanding work performance and drive. They hoped that Mark, in view of his younger age and creativity, would add still more drive to the post, as they had come to think that old John, the former Manager of the Red Pot, although an old hand in the industry, had become rather conservative as the years had gone by.

The Ocean Hotel has a very tight system to control sales performance of each restaurant. Every restaurant manager has to prepare sales forecast monthly, quarterly and yearly. They are also fully responsible to reach the sales target which is jointly set by the restaurant manager and top management. Restaurant managers are also expected to provide weekly performance report to top management and provide fully explanations if the sales is below forecast. Mark often considered that there were too much paperwork for him.

The staff thought that Mark had become high-handed after his promotion. He was not diplomatic enough when giving orders or assigning tasks. As he felt insecure in his new post, he had introduced a new range of rewards and punishments in order to gain better sales promotion, hospitality, service, etc. These ideas had originally been introduced to improve staff performance, but the system was too rigid and unreasonable. Mark had been nicknamed "watchdog" by his staff behind his back. Moreover, Mark enjoyed flattery from his staff, and with those who indulged him in this, he was exceptionally easy-going.

Furthermore, Mark put on airs, pulled long faces and was intolerant of any of the staff's constructive opinions. His stringent management style resulted in the staff becoming very tense in their work. His subordinates found their hands tied and feared breaking the rules. Unhappy with their situation, staff resigned one after the other and long-time customers failed to come as they used to.

The top management and the Food and Beverage Director discussed the prospects of Red Pot Restaurant in their biweekly meetings and finally concluded that Mark was the "culprit" behind the worsening situation. Mark was invited to a discussion with Jonathan, the Food and Beverage Director. Jonathan put the case squarely to Mark, deliberately avoiding mentioning the names of any of his subordinates who had revealed the true state of affairs. Mark was invited back a few times afterwards. He even sat once with the top management on the board. As before, he showed a sense of cooperation and kind heartiness to his staff. He said that he was very lenient on his staff and had fully considered their feelings.

Mark's famous speech when being questioned by senior management was: "I am fully aware of the shortage of high-quality restaurant staff in Hong Kong. There is no reason for me to ill-treat my boys and girls. I am sure that there is some misunderstanding with my boys and girls. I will try to iron out the differences."

When Mark returned to his office, he behaved entirely differently towards his staff. He continued to abuse his power and ordered them around. He became even harsher than before. The relationship between

Mark and his subordinates grew tenser. Now that he had to control the deteriorating situation in the outlet virtually alone, he was under pressure to work harder in the new hostile situation around him, and as new faces kept appearing, his past high spirits and drive gradually deserted him. Under the stress, his former good temper turned to moodiness and sudden outbursts of temper, and at times, he shouted even at the customers as well as his subordinates.

Furthermore, his relationship with his girlfriend, Diane, had also worsened, and this aggravated his situation still more, since Diane had been his main support.

Jonathan called in Mark and reminded him on the importance of being in a good and relieved mood both towards himself and his working environment. Nevertheless, the situation persisted, and a few months later, the top management finally decided to replace him. Being unsuccessful to locate a suitable job for Mark within the hotel chain, Mark's contract was terminated afterwards. They knew it was a tragedy to Mark, a promising young man, and realigned that it might cast a shadow on the whole of his future career.

Questions for Discussion

1. Why did Mark Lee change his working attitudes?
2. If you were Jonathan, the Food and Beverage Director, how would you help Mark to become an effective Restaurant Manager?
3. Can the hotel top management review some of its systems such as promotion criteria, sales performance monitoring etc. to prevent similar incident to happen in the future?

17

Lost and Found: The Wallet of Jones

C. Lok

The Harbour Hotel, a part of an international hotel chain, is a five-star hotel in Hong Kong. Over 90% of its guests are business professionals visiting Hong Kong for various business purposes including attending conferences, exhibitions and other business functions. With an average room rate of HK$2,500–3,500, the hotel has to maintain a very high quality of customer service to its guests. The motto for the international office is "The Customer is Number One!"

Daisy Yip, the front office duty manager of The Harbour Hotel, has held the job for the last three years. Having joined the hotel for seven years, she knows the operation of the hotel very well. She is also praised by her supervisors as the most organized staff. In the last three years, she was highly commended for the high-quality customer service to the hotel guests.

One day at about 11:00 a.m., Daisy received an urgent fax from Singapore (see Figure 1).

When Daisy received the fax and remembering that David Jones was a senior executive of a Fortune 100 Company in the United States, she immediately checked the logbook of the housekeeper for the 16th floor. The room had been cleaned by a room attendant at 4:30 a.m. The room attendant, Mrs. Liu, has been doing the same job for two years with the hotel. She has a good record and maintained a good standard in her work. The room had then been checked by Mrs. Wong, the floor supervisor for the past six years. After her check, she would then enter into the logbook whether there was anything special, including

Figure 1: The First Urgent Fax from David Jones

American Instruments
Singapore Inc.
1 Orchid Road
Singapore

14 Dec. 1997

The Duty Manager
The Harbour Hotel
Harbour Road
Hong Kong

Dear Sir,

I checked out of your hotel at 4:00 a.m. today. During the past week, I was staying in Room 1601.

When I arrived in Singapore at 10:30 a.m., I discovered that my black wallet was still in the safe in my room. All my credit cards and citizen card are in the wallet and I cannot survive without them. Could you please send the wallet to me at the above address by courier service (foreign collect) as soon as possible?

Thank you for your assistance.

Yours faithfully,

David Jones

customer items, left behind. The standard procedure to look for guest items left behind was for the duty manager to check the logbook in the housekeeping department. Unless there was anything unusual, she would not contact the housekeeping staff who usually work in shifts. During the past three years, Daisy has handled over 300 enquiries of lost items of guests, and 99% could be located in the housekeeping department after checking the logbook.

Daisy looked at the logbook this time but found nothing unusual with Room 1601. She therefore sent a reply to Mr. David Jones at 12:00 p.m. to say that the black wallet had not been found in room cleaning.

At 3:00 p.m., she received another urgent fax from David Jones (see Figure 2).

Daisy, after reading the fax, immediately talked with Mrs. Wong and intended to check Room 1601 again. Unfortunately, the room was occupied by another guest and while this guest occupied the room, the hotel staff had no authority to open the safe.

David Jones called at 5:00 p.m. sharp. Daisy explained the situation to him and promised to take further action as soon as the guest returned. Jones was annoyed and warned that he would not stay in the hotel again unless the wallet was found. He had the impression someone has put away the wallet or used the credit cards illegally.

The guest of Room 1601 returned at late 11:30 p.m.

The safe was then opened by the guest in the presence of Mrs. Wong and the guest services manager. A small black wallet was found in the top compartment.

Questions for Discussion

1. What are the possible reasons the wallet was not discovered by either the room attendant or the supervisor?
2. What should duty manager have done before replying to David Jones's first fax?
3. If you were the housekeeping manager, what steps would you take to ensure the same case would not happen again?

Figure 2: The Second Urgent Fax from David Jones

American Instruments
Singapore Inc.
1 Orchid Road
Singapore

14 Dec. 1997

Ms. Daisy Yip
The Harbour Hotel
Harbour Road
Hong Kong

Dear Ms. Yip,

I was very surprised that my wallet could not be located. I am pretty sure that it was in the safe.

Have you done a real search?

I shall call you within the next two hours to clarify the situation.

Sincerely yours

David Jones

Part VII

Occupational Safety

18

The Lost Fingers

C. Lok and R. Lee

William Lee, the Human Resources Manager of a well-known restaurant chain in Hong Kong, is sitting in his office and completing the last part of Mrs. Chan Yuk-fun's personal file. He has been working on this file for two and a half years and wished to put it in the personal record cabinet forever. He did not want to recall the tragic story of Yuk-fun any more.

William has worked with the Golden-Bird Restaurant Group for nine years. When the Group was still a small enterprise nine years ago, William was responsible for the recruitment of all levels of staff, from senior management to cleaners, and kitchen helpers. Yuk-fun had been employed by William as a kitchen helper of one of the restaurants six years ago.

She was first assigned for washing dishes in the stewarding department for three and a half years and was later transferred to the pastry kitchen. The tragedy took place soon after she had just officially worked as an apprentice in the kitchen for one or two weeks.

One day she was washing a grinder with a brush with a long handle. She was wearing two pairs of gloves, a pair of labourers' gloves and a pair of tube gloves. She was cleaning the grinder with a piece of cloth when it was still switched on. Suddenly, the force of the grinder pulled both the piece of cloth and her gloves inside it. Overwhelmed by the sudden incident, she immediately yelled. A worker nearby who noticed the accident rushed forward and switched off the grinder but it was already too late. The grinder had jammed the ring finger and the little finger of her left hand. She felt the great pain immediately and noticed that the gloves were torn and blood kept pouring out, covering the area. It had taken a long time for her to loosen her binders, with the painstaking effort of her colleagues. The kitchen was in chaos, with both helpers and chefs dashing to try to stop the bleeding. Yuk-fun was then rushed to a nearby hospital for treatment.

The incident was by no means final. Yuk-fun had to be hospitalized for a long period and had to undergo numerous operations, some of which were complicated involving transplanting flesh from her thigh onto her broken fingers. Her movement in the hospital was entirely restricted. The treatment had lasted for over two years. After hospitalization, she had to go over follow-up treatment and physiotherapy. Every week she had to travel long distance from her Kowloon residence to the hospital on Hong Kong Island. It took twice a week and she had to be scouted by her family to the hospital. Not to mention the comfort and visits from the restaurant employer. In the period, both parties involved suffered tremendously.

As Yuk-fun was an employee of the restaurant, she was under the insurance coverage of the restaurant chain. Since she was injured during work (although by self-negligence), she applied for compensation for an industrial injury from the Labour Department. At first she was considered to have 15% disability of her left hand. Through labour tribunal judgment it was determined that her left hand had 20% permanent injury. She finally received a compensation of HK$750,000 which included also a substantial sum for her sufferings. During the two years' period, she received 100% salary from the restaurant.

During the period covering her accident and its after-effects, the restaurant transferred her to fill a vacancy in the laundry section. She had to handle the fitter and folder machine in the section. Although it meant simple chores, she had to stand all the time and she could not work with ease with her broken fingers. Upon receiving the large sum of compensation she resigned.

Question for Discussion

Who is (are) responsible for the accident?

Class Adoption

We shall provide a free inspection copy to each teaching professional who is interested in reviewing our titles in this series for adoption in his courses. Supplementary materials, such as Teaching Notes, will also be provided free if the titles have been adopted. However, The Chinese University Press reserves the right to refuse request for complimentary copies which are not within its complimentary copy policy.

For inspection copies, please write using your institution's letterhead indicating your class size and the intended adoption date to:

Business Manager
The Chinese University Press
The Chinese University of Hong Kong
Sha Tin
New Territories
Hong Kong
Telephone: (852) 2609 6508 / 2609 6500
Facsimile: (852) 2603 6692 / 2603 7355

MANAGEMENT DEVELOPMENT SERIES

Already published

Hong Kong Management Cases in Hotel Management

Hong Kong Management Cases in Information Systems Management

Hong Kong Management Cases in Marketing

專業管理叢書

即將出版

《香港市場管理學個案選輯》

已刊書目

《香港及國內管理個案選輯》

《香港商業法》

《組織行為與人事管理》

《管理人經濟學》

《管理資訊系統》

《管理學原理》

《數量方法的管理應用》

The Case Study Group of Hong Kong

The Case Study Group of Hong Kong was formed in 1987 with the objective of promoting case method for management teaching and training in the territory. With administrative and advisory support from The Management Development Centre of Hong Kong, the Group has regular meetings and seminars during which cases are presented.

The Case Study Group is open to those in Hong Kong who are involved in the use of case materials and methods in management training and development (whether by occupation or interest).

If you will complete the details below, we will add your name to our mailing list and notify you of all forthcoming activities.

Name (Last, First):	
HKID No.:	
Job Title:	
Company Name:	
Company Address:	
Home Address:	
Telephone (office):	
Fax (office):	
Specialized area:	

Please return to:
Ms. May Li
The Management Development Centre of Hong Kong,
11/F., VTC Tower, 27 Wood Road, Wan Chai,
Hong Kong

Tel : 2836 1818
Fax : 2572 7130

Annual Case Writing Competition

Write to Win

Since 1988, The Management Development Centre of Hong Kong has started organizing the Annual Case Writer of the Year Competitions. With the sponsorship of the American Chamber of Commerce Charitable Foundation, the competitions have been most successful and attracted a large number of good quality case submission every year.

For further information about the Case Writing Competition, please call or write to the Executive Officer of The Management Development Centre of Hong Kong at 11/F., VTC Tower, 27 Wood Road, Wan Chai, Hong Kong (Tel: 2836 1816, Fax: 2572 7130).